AMERICA'S MOST WANTED RECIPES

Restaurant Favorites Your Family's
Pickiest Eaters Will Love

KIDS' MENU

Also by Ron Douglas

America's Most Wanted Recipes

More of America's Most Wanted Recipes

America's Most Wanted Recipes Without the Guilt

America's Most Wanted Recipes Just Desserts

America's Most Wanted Recipes At The Grill

AMERICA'S MOST WANTED RECIPES

Restaurant Favorites Your Family's Pickiest Eaters Will Love

KIDS' MENU

RON DOUGLAS

ATRIA PAPERBACK

NEW YORK • LONDON • TORONTO • SYDNEY • NEW DELHI

ATRIA PAPERBACK
An Imprint of Simon & Schuster, Inc.
1230 Avenue of the Americas
New York, NY 10020

First Atria Paperback edition June 2015

ATRIA PAPERBACK and colophon are trademarks of Simon & Schuster, Inc.

For information about special discounts for bulk purchases, please contact Simon & Schuster Special Sales at 1-866-506-1949 or business@simonandschuster.com.

The Simon & Schuster Speakers Bureau can bring authors to your live event. For more information or to book an event, contact the Simon & Schuster Speakers Bureau at 1-866-248-3049 or visit our website at www.simonspeakers.com.

Interior design by Davina Mock-Maniscalco

Manufactured in the United States of America

10 9 8 7 6 5 4 3 2 1

Library of Congress Cataloging-in-Publication Data is available.

ISBN 978-1-4767-3491-0
ISBN 978-1-4767-3492-7 (ebook)

*To Nia and Ryan, words cannot
express how much Daddy loves you.*

CONTENTS

INTRODUCTION

It may surprise some of you, but I don't actually spend *all* my time coming up with copycat recipes. By day, I manage and taste test and sit down at my desk to write things like this introduction. But the rest of my time and energy is spent being a dad.

Right now the house is quiet. I've just dropped the kids off at camp, leaving me time to focus on this book, the latest in the *America's Most Wanted Recipes* series, and reflect the special place it has in my heart. After five books and 1.2 million copies worldwide, I felt sure this one should feature dishes that kids love, that they look forward to eating when they dine out with their families. It was my son and daughter, after all, who inspired me to leave the corporate world years ago to become a cookbook author—to teach other parents around the world how to prepare the restaurant meals their families enjoy but in the warm comfort of their homes. I wanted to be the dad to my kids that I wished I'd had growing up.

In 1971, there was a pretty young girl from a rough area of Queens, New York, named Sharon. Like many teenagers, Sharon started hanging out with the wrong crowd and made some poor decisions, one of which was succumbing to peer pressure that led to recreational drug use. At that time, New York City was a lot different than it is now. The streets were flooded with heroin, and the crime rate was one of the highest in the country. By the mid-70s an estimated 200,000 people abused heroin in New York City. Sharon's drug use eventually led to heroin addiction as well.

In 1972, her parents checked her in to a rehabilitation clinic in Harlem to get help. It was there that she met a handsome and charming young man from Yonkers named Ronald. Ronald's reason for being in rehab was a bit different. He was a heroin user as well, but he was also a dealer. At that time, Ronald was involved in one of the biggest drug busts in Westchester County history with several mob-associated gangsters indicted. He pleaded down in court to being a user and got sentenced to attend rehab as part of his plea deal.

Sharon and Ronald became good friends while in rehab and supported each other's efforts to get clean. They eventually started dating and fell in love. It was a happy time for them. In April of 1974, they got married—she was only nineteen years old, and he was just twenty.

In August of that same year, while expecting their first child, Ronald went missing for several days and Sharon could not get in contact with him. Ever since they had been together, he had never gone more than a day without at least calling her. She feared for the worst. A few days later, she got a call from the police informing her that Ronald had been found dead on a rooftop in Harlem. Evidently his past had caught up with him. When they found him, he was badly beaten and overdosed with heroin. It was thought to be a homicide, but police never discovered who did it.

So there was Sharon, a nineteen-year-old, newly-wedded, pregnant mother who had just lost her husband. Life had dealt her a cruel blow. Six weeks later in October 1974, she gave birth to a baby boy whom she would name after her lost love, Ronald.

If you haven't guessed by now, Sharon is my mother, I am Ronald Jr., and this is how my life story began. Having been born in October 1974, I missed meeting my dad by about six weeks. My mother spent the early years of my life in a deep depression after losing her first love so suddenly. She relapsed into heavy drug use. Much of my childhood was spent living at my grandparents' house without seeing my mom for days at a time. I would often sit by the window crying, waiting for her to come home. Statistically, I had a slim chance of succeeding in life. Neither genetics nor environment was on my side. The pain from my early years motivated me to never do drugs, and I promised myself that my kids would never have to go through what I did.

Fast-forward to 2004. I married the love of my life, and my daughter, Nia, was born. I had a good job on Wall Street working for JPMorgan Chase and we had just bought our first home. Everything seemed perfect, but it wasn't. I was working sixty to eighty hours a week and the only time I'd get to see my daughter was for an hour or so at night and on the weekends. The best part of my day was coming home and hearing her precious little voice yell out, "Daddy is home!" before she went to bed. I wanted to provide for her, but I felt like I was becoming the absentee dad I had vowed not to be.

That was the realization I needed. In 2007, a month before my son, Ryan, was born, I finally decided to leave the rat race for good and focus on RecipeSecrets.net and *America's Most Wanted Recipes* full-time. Since then I've had the freedom to be home with the kids and play an active role in their lives.

And if you're wondering, my mother has cleaned up her act and is an awesome grandmother. She spoils them rotten, and our family bond has never been stronger. She has taught me what it's like to overcome adversity and survive whatever hard times life sends your way. She was also my inspiration in the kitchen having shown me the fundamentals of cooking at an early age.

I truly hope that *America's Most Wanted Recipes Kids' Menu,* as well as the other books in the *America's Most Wanted Recipes* series, brings you as much joy as it's given me.

About *America's Most Wanted Recipes Kids' Menu*

This cookbook features 114 recipes inspired by the most popular kids' menu dishes served in leading restaurants across the country, according to our market research, which includes poll data from RecipeSecrets.net members. Each recipe has been tested and tweaked to taste just like the original. Armed with these instructions, you can now skip the wait while eating out and impress your family and friends by making these dishes at home whenever you want.

If you've read any of my other books or visited RecipeSecrets.net, you know that I've made a career out of creating copycat versions of popular restaurant dishes. They're delicious, for sure, but not exactly health food. With childhood obesity growing at an alarming rate, I'd be remiss if I didn't use this opportunity and the platform I have to provide some important information that parents can use to improve their kids' eating habits.

It is up to us as parents to regulate our children's diets and to ensure that restaurant-style dishes are reserved for an occasional treat. The recipes in this cookbook are perfect for that purpose and are also fun to re-create at home and compare against the original version. As a responsible father of two young kids, I don't recommend them as a part of your kids' regular diet. The good news is, by making these dishes at home, you have the option to make them healthier by substituting different ingredients and cooking methods.

I encourage you to read our Guide to Kids' Nutrition on the following pages and to keep your kids' health and development in mind as you enjoy these recipes.

Ron Douglas
RecipeSecrets.net
Find us on Facebook: www.facebook.com/LikeRecipeSecrets

AMERICA'S MOST WANTED RECIPES

Restaurant Favorites Your Family's Pickiest Eaters Will Love

KIDS' MENU

A GUIDE TO KIDS' NUTRITION

The foods we eat today will affect our health tomorrow and in the years to come. Good nutrition is a key to leading a healthy and happy life and can reduce our risk of heart disease, cancer, diabetes, and high blood pressure. We have all heard these things a million times before, and for the most part, we all know how our diets can affect our daily lives.

But what about our children? Do they know? They should! It is our job as parents to educate our children on good nutrition. It is our job as parents to feed our children healthy food that can reduce their risk of chronic diseases later in life. Our children look to us for guidance, and their health is our responsibility.

> *Today, more than 95% of all chronic disease is caused by food choice, toxic food ingredients, nutritional deficiencies and lack of physical exercise.*
>
> *—Mike Adams*

What Is Proper Nutrition?

Why do we eat? To fill up our tummies? To satisfy a craving? Some would say yes, but it is so much more than that. Food provides us with nutrition in order to maintain life and growth. Proper nutrition is providing ourselves with the nutrients needed to build our bodies and give ourselves the energy we need. To do this we must consume the necessary nutrients to grow muscle, support bone density, encourage proper cell development, support our body's immune system, and develop brain functions. These are all necessary to grow children into strong and healthy adults.

The Difference Between Adult Nutritional Needs and Children's Nutritional Needs

A child's body is very different than an adult's. Yes, our children may look like miniature versions of us, but because they are still growing and developing, they have different nutritional requirements than we do. This is true from infancy all the way through the teen years. Our children are growing in ways we cannot see, and good nutrition is vital to their overall growth and development. They also have a higher metabolic rate than adults.

One common misconception is that children should have separate menus or "kid food" that can and should be enjoyed until adulthood. *Then* they can begin eating better, right? Not true. Most foods aimed at children are full of chemicals and empty calories. They are processed foods that contain little to no nutritional value. This means the foods we are feeding our children are inadequate and not supporting their growth and development. They are instead promoting poor eating habits that, when not corrected, can carry into adulthood.

A child's body does not need empty calories, it needs nutritious food. A survey completed recently by Kidshealth.org found that one in three children in America is overweight or obese. Why? Because typically their diet consists of processed and fast foods instead of fruits, vegetables, and other whole foods. When a child's nutritional needs are not being met, they may be unable to perform at age-appropriate levels. Children do have a higher metabolic rate, which means they require more calories than adults do, but these calories must be of good nutritional value.

Different Nutritional Needs at Different Developmental Stages

A child's nutritional needs and calorie recommendations will vary depending on their age. Toddlers and preschoolers will require between 1,300 and 1,800 calories a day. After your toddler's first birthday, you may notice him becoming picky about what he eats. Children this age may resist mealtime. It is also a time when they are the most impressionable. For this reason, it is important to model healthy eating habits.

Toddlers and preschoolers grow at a slower rate than they did as infants. They need enough calories to maintain their energy level, but they do not need adult-size portions. Servings for a child this age should be about a third the size for an adult. Don't force a child at this age to clear their plate. When they say they are done, let it be. Avoid foods with large amounts of sugar like desserts, soft drinks, sugar-coated cereals, chips, and candy. These foods have little to no nutritional value.

Toddlers should eat the following amount of foods each day:

- Whole grains: about 1½ ounces. Examples of what this size serving looks like are 1 slice of bread, ½ cup cereal, 3 whole wheat crackers, or ½ cup cooked pasta.
- Vegetables: 2 to 3 tablespoons
- Fruits: ½ to ¾ cup
- Dairy: 1 to 1½ cups
- Meat/protein: about 2 ounces a day. Examples of what this size serving looks like are 1 egg, 1 tablespoon peanut butter, or a slice of turkey.

School-age children need around 2,000 calories a day. These calories should come from a minimum of 2 to 3 servings of fruit and 3 to 4 servings of vegetables a day, as well as a balanced diet including protein, dairy, and whole grains.

Meeting Nutritional Requirements

Children who are actively involved in sports will require more calories. The suggested amount of calories for your child is just that—a suggestion. Children who are typically high-energy may require more, while those who are not as active may require less. Regardless, all calories should come from nutritious sources.

Another important thing to consider when meeting your child's nutritional requirements is variety. When considering variety in terms of your child's diet, don't think of how often or how much a child may eat certain foods. Instead, consider what range of food options they choose to eat. Children should be encouraged to eat a variety of whole foods to foster a balanced diet.

Making fruits and vegetables part of the main course will ensure your child is getting a variety of vitamins, minerals, and fiber. This will facilitate healthy growth from a young age.

The Food Groups

Let's take a look at the different food groups.

Dairy: Dairy foods are rich in nutrients that help strengthen your bones. These include potassium, calcium, and vitamin D. Research has found that including dairy products into your diet can reduce risk of cardiovascular disease and type 2 diabetes and lower blood pressure in adults.

Fruits and Vegetables: Fruits and vegetables should make up about half of your plate at mealtime. Fruits are an excellent source of vitamins, minerals, and fiber. Vegetables are also loaded with nutrients. Diets that include a large amount of vegetables can help reduce the risk of heart disease, stroke, type 2 diabetes, and some types of cancer.

Grains: This includes breads, cereals, and potatoes. According to the My Plate Guide (choosemyplate.gov), around 25% of your plate should be grains. Half of your grain servings should come from whole grains. These are a great source of B vitamins, fiber, and magnesium. These nutrients work together to reduce the risk of heart disease and diabetes.

Protein: This includes meat, poultry, fish, and alternate sources like peanut butter. Around 25% of your plate should be high-protein foods. Protein is an important component of body tissues, blood, and hormones. It also supports muscle tone.

The Importance of a Good Foundation in Healthy Eating

There are a variety of reasons to give our children a good foundation in healthy eating. A healthy diet can provide a boost to our children's immune systems. A child's immune system is underdeveloped. This means that they can be more prone to infections. Zinc and magnesium are two important components that can support the immune system.

Children also need an adequate amount of carbohydrate in their diets. Children have high energy levels and providing them just enough carbs can give them the energy they need throughout their day.

A diet full of healthy foods like fruits, vegetables, and whole grains will meet all these nutritional requirements and can provide a good foundation for your child's overall health.

Proper nutrition can play a role in brain development, behavior, attention span, and your child's risk of health problems like asthma, obesity, heart disease, and more.

Children who do not eat healthfully can have difficulty learning in school, misbehave, feel sluggish or tired, or experience the opposite effect and be hyperactive. They may struggle with obesity, or be too skinny and malnourished. Poor nutrition can affect a child's sleep patterns, social development, and ability to focus.

What does this boil down to? Sometimes children who have poor nutrition are simply unable to function. Think of it in terms of your automobile. If you fill up your gas tank with water, the tank may be full, but it is not going to go. You must provide it with the proper fuel. Our children's bodies are the same. They must be armed with the proper nutrition if we want them to grow and thrive.

Another consideration is how food can affect your energy level. If you eat too much or too little, you may feel sluggish. Or, if you eat food containing lots of sugar you may feel a burst of energy but will lose it just as quickly. If foods affect you that way, how much more do they affect our children?

If a child has a well-balanced diet, they will feel more energetic and will be better prepared to conquer the tasks they face throughout the day.

Other Factors That Affect Children's Health

There are so many reasons that proper nutrition is important in the daily lives of our children, but nutrition is not the only factor that can affect their health. Here are some others:

Sleep

Sleep or lack of it is another area that researchers say may be linked to obesity. Parents tend to be busy and sleep deprived, so it is natural that children may be getting less rest than they need. Modeling and encouraging healthy sleeping habits can be done in a few different ways. Make sure you know what amount of sleep your child should be getting.

- 1–3 years need 12–14 hours a day
- 3–5 years need 11–13 hours a day
- 5–10 years need 10–11 hours a day

Children should have a regular bedtime routine each night. They should also go to bed and wake up at the same time every day. This helps their bodies get into a pattern of rest. Rooms should be quiet, dark, and relaxing and should be free of distractions like TVs, computers, or other electronics. Many families like to read books or turn on soothing music to help children wind down before bed.

Reducing screen time is crucial and one healthy habit that should not be ignored. At home, parents can pull the plug on electronics by limiting the amount of screen time children have. The goal is no more than 2 hours of screen time a day for young children. Have activities ready indoors on days when you are unable to go outside. These could include crafts, puzzles, or board games.

Physical Activity

Physical activity is crucial to the health of children. There are many ways to encourage children to be physically active. Schools can make sure that gym classes are not cut due to budget cuts. Recess is important, and this time should be honored. At home, parents are in charge of how much physical activity a child has. Children should be encouraged to go outside and play. If you live in an urban area, then you should go for walks with your children. Visit parks or indoor play areas. Children should be physically active for a minimum of 60 minutes a day. This activity should be of moderate to vigorous intensity and should be developmentally appropriate. Here are some examples of physical activity that the whole family can enjoy.

Indoor

- Put on a play by acting out your child's favorite book.
- Allow your child to help with chores like dusting or vacuuming.
- Have an indoor treasure hunt by hiding an item in your house and using a map to find it.
- Play indoor basketball using a soft foam ball. You can use a laundry basket as a hoop!
- Have a dance party! Mix it up by also freeze dancing. When the music stops, everyone has to stop and hold his position until it starts again.

Outdoor

- Winter activities can include building a snowman, making snow angels, or sledding.
- Play games like ring-around-the-rosy, hide-and-seek, the hokey-pokey, and tag.
- Throw, roll, or kick balls in the backyard.
- Take a nature walk.
- Go to the park.

Oral Health

Another thing to consider is your child's oral health. Teeth that are exposed to sugar frequently throughout the day are more likely to develop tooth decay. This is because the sugars are digested by bacteria in our mouths and converted to acid. The acid initiates the decay process in teeth; those that are exposed to sugar more often will cause the decay to progress further.

The Childhood Obesity Epidemic

Childhood obesity rates in the United States have tripled over the past 30 years. The percentage of obese children ages 6 to 11 years in the United States went up from 7% in 1980 to 18% in 2012. This means that today close to one in three children in this country is obese or overweight. The numbers are higher (nearly 40%) in Hispanic and African American communities.

The term "overweight" means having excess body weight for a particular height from any combination of fat, muscle, bone, or water. The term "obesity" is defined as being overweight plus having excess body fat. Typically, a person becomes overweight or obese due to a caloric imbalance, meaning too few calories "worked off" compared to the amount of calories consumed. This can also be affected by genetic, behavioral, and environmental factors.

If our country does not find a way to solve this epidemic, a third of all children born will suffer from diabetes, high blood pressure, asthma, or other obesity-related health problems at some point in their lives.

The Effects of Childhood Obesity

Childhood obesity has immediate and long-term consequences on a child's health and well-being.

Immediate Health Effects

- Children who are considered obese are at higher risk of cardiovascular disease, high cholesterol, and high blood pressure.
- A population-based sample from the CDC showed that 70% of obese children between 5 and 17 were at risk of cardiovascular disease.
- Adolescents who are obese are more likely to have prediabetes, meaning their blood glucose levels indicate they have a high risk of developing diabetes.
- Obese children are at higher risk of developing bone and joint problems, sleep apnea, and poor self-esteem.

Long-Term Health Effects

- A child who is obese is likely to continue with obesity into adulthood. This means they are at greater risk of adult health problems like heart disease, stroke, type 2 diabetes, and osteoarthritis.

- Being overweight or obese is also associated with certain types of cancers like breast, esophageal, thyroid, gallbladder, ovarian, and others.

How It Happened

The rate of childhood obesity has skyrocketed over the past 30 years. Many wonder why now? And how did this happen? The answers vary, but for the most part our children's lives are much different than ours were 30 years ago. Decades ago, kids walked to school, had recess and gym class, and played outside for hours after school. Many meals were home-cooked and had reasonable portion sizes and included vegetables. Eating out and snacking between meals was a rare occurrence.

Life for today's children is much different. Children now ride a bus or are driven to school. Gym classes are rare due to budget cuts, and afternoons are spent watching TV, playing video games, or browsing the web. Many times both parents work and life is busy. This leads to fewer home-cooked meals at home.

Snacking all day has become a common occurrence. Children 30 years ago typically ate one snack a day; the trend now is three snacks. This results in an additional 200 calories a day. Our portion sizes have also gone up. Compared to years past, portions are now two to five times bigger. Another thing that has gone up is beverage portions. In the mid-1970s the average sugar-sweetened drink was 13.6 ounces. Today's kids typically drink 20 ounces. This adds up to around 31% more calories than was typical 40 years ago. These additional calories include 56% more fats and oils and 14% more sugar. Compared to the average American in 1970, we now eat around 15 more pounds of sugar a year.

Our children are also spending a lot more time using entertainment media. The average 17-year-old spends 7½ hours a day using electronics. This includes video games, cell phones, movies, TV, and computers. Only one-third of high school students are getting the recommended level of physical activity each day.

Serving and Portion Sizes

Before we begin discussing the problem with serving and portion sizes, it is important to understand what the terms mean. A serving size is a specific amount of food or drink that is defined by measurements such as cups, tablespoons, or ounces. Portion sizes are the amount of food that happens to end up on a plate. Portion sizes are the actual amount of food kids eat at mealtime. They can be bigger or smaller than the recommended serving size.

While we can blame obesity partly on unhealthy food and little physical activity, another large factor is the growing portion size, which began rising in the 1980s. Over time, our perception of accurate food portion has increased so much that we now have become largely unaware of how much food we really need.

When you look at the serving size on a label it is important to realize that it is an estimation. It is not an accurate amount of how much a child should have. Typically, the serving size is targeted at adults, not children. It also tells you how much nutrition you are getting from the food, but not how much you should eat.

A more accurate way to tell how much kids should be eating is to look at the United States Department of Agriculture's (USDA) My Plate website (choosemyplate.gov). My Plate provides recommendations that are based on the government's dietary guidelines. It can help parents and adults recognize accurate serving sizes, and can help children visualize appropriate portion sizes. When looking at your plate you should visualize it divided into four equal sections. The top quarter of the plate would be used for protein, the other top quarter would be for grains (preferably whole grains), and the bottom half of the plate could be divided up between fruit and/or vegetables. By visualizing your plate in sections, you and your children will be able to get a better idea of appropriate portion sizes.

Additional tips to help with portion sizes are:

- Serve meals on smaller plates. This makes a meal look larger.
- If they must have snacks like chips or ice cream, it's best to limit them to individual portions. Don't allow children to serve themselves unhealthy snacks.

- At restaurants, offer to split meals. Many times restaurant portions are larger than necessary.
- Don't expect kids to clean their plates. Many times children as young as preschool age do a better job controlling their portion sizes than adults do.
- Teach your children to visualize food servings as everyday objects. For example, a serving of rice would be the same as an ice cream scoop. A serving of meat should be the size of a deck of cards. A serving of bread would be the same as a CD cover.

The statistics are staggering, and honestly a little overwhelming. Fixing the childhood obesity epidemic can seem daunting. But we have the tools available to fight it, and with some lifestyle changes, we can help our children lead healthier lives.

Be the Role Model

As parents, we are the role models for our children. We put the food on the table, and we play a pivotal role in what our children eat. If our children see us eating healthy foods, they are going to want to eat them too. If we live a sedentary lifestyle and sit on the couch with a bag of potato chips . . . our children may follow suit.

In a recent survey provided by WebMD, 70% of children under the age of 12 said they would talk to their parents about nutrition and body size. The majority of the children surveyed also ranked mom and dad as their highest nutritional role models.

What does this mean? It means that we parents must model the appropriate behavior and nutrition habits for our children. We cannot expect them to eat healthy foods, exercise, and watch portion sizes if we don't. We must model what's best for them if we want our children to live long, healthy lives.

Schools can also play a huge role in helping children establish healthy habits. They should provide opportunities for their students to learn about healthy eating and the importance of physical activity.

Childcare centers can often opt into nutritious food programs, called Child and Adult Care Food Programs (CACFP). Many of these programs reimburse childcare centers for purchasing healthy food. They also offer nutrition training for childcare providers and administrators. For information regarding these programs in your state, check the USDA directory.

Another way to model healthy habits is to change the way we look at celebrations. Holidays and parties tend to focus on food. We Americans have gotten in the habit of "stuffing" ourselves in the name of a celebration. Modeling healthy habits is important, and these can easily start with changing the foods we serve during special occasions.

Apple slices with peanut butter or yogurt, veggies and fruit served with dip, graham crackers or animal crackers, baked chips and salsa, and water flavored with citrus fruits are all great options. So is packing party favor bags with nonedible items like pencils, bookmarks, or stickers.

How to Get Your Children to Want to Eat Healthier

Many parents may truly want their children to eat healthier, but their kids balk at the idea of fruits and vegetables, and may just be downright picky! If this is your family, you are not alone. It is hard to change food habits in adults, let alone a finicky child. However, good nutrition is important, and it is our job to make our children eat healthier, whether they want to or not. However, a child who wants to is a lot easier than one who doesn't.

One way to get your child to want to eat healthier is by being honest with them. This works best with older, school-age children. Many children this age have already had basic nutrition in schools and have some sort of idea what it means. Talk to your children about how we truly are "what we eat." If they want to grow strong and be healthy, they must eat healthy foods. Talk about the fact that what they eat will affect them later in life. Mention lightly the diseases that unhealthy eating can cause. Be real, but be gentle. Consider your conversation and make sure it is age appropriate.

Get your children involved! Take them to a farmers' market and let them pick out fruits and vegetables. Build a garden of your own, and let them decide on what to plant. Let the kids wash and prepare the vegetables when you get home from the grocery store. Let them cut fruits and vegetables into fun shapes, or serve them with a tasty dip. Apples can be served with peanut butter; celery can turn into "ants on a log" by using peanut butter and raisins. Carrot sticks can be dipped into ranch dressing. Using a cookie cutter, transform watermelon slices into stars, or pineapples into hearts. You can also make "fruit kebabs" using a skewer and fruit shapes. This is a fun snack with a twist that kids will love!

Another thing to do with younger children is talk to them about the rainbow of nutrients. Throughout the day, we should be eating a rainbow of colors. Each color of food represents a special nutrient. Tell them that if they only eat apples and grapes, they won't get the nutrients found in blueberries and strawberries. If they only eat the orange carrots, they will be missing out on the nutrients found in green veggies like broccoli and green beans. Even young children can understand the concept of the rainbow. Be honest, and consider your child's age when you discuss nutrients. You can go as in depth as your child is ready for.

Make healthy eating a family affair! Challenge your whole family to try one new fruit or vegetable every week.

One thing that is very important when it comes to getting your children to eat healthy is DO NOT GIVE UP! Some children may need to try a new food up to 20 times before they realize they like it. This is a battle of wills and many parents may give up, thinking their child will never like the food. Remember trying something new takes time, and old habits are hard to break. Keep introducing the food, and eventually your child may learn to like it.

How to Eat Healthier at Home

One way to ensure your family will be eating healthier is by offering healthier food at home. As parents, we are 100 percent responsible for food that is brought into our homes and served to our families.

> *You don't have to cook fancy or complicated masterpieces—just good food from fresh ingredients.*
>
> —*Julia Child*

Better Ingredients

All it takes are a few healthy ingredient substitutions to transform your diet from unhealthy to very nutritious. Try these out. I guarantee you that you will instantly reduce fat, salt, calories, and sugar in your diet and not a bit of flavor. Instead of

- White bread, try whole-grain breads
- Using butter to keep food from sticking, try cooking spray or nonstick pans
- Bacon, try Canadian or turkey bacon
- Ground beef, try ground turkey
- Whole milk, drink fat-free or low-fat
- White rice or pasta, try whole-grain or wheat pasta
- Canned fruit in heavy syrup, buy water- or juice-packed canned fruits
- Using the whole amount of sugar the recipe calls for, try cutting it in half or reducing it by one-quarter
- Seasoning salts, use fresh herbs and spices

Fresh fruit and vegetables are always the healthiest option. Next would be frozen. If something is out of season or unavailable, or if you can't find it in the freezer aisle, buying canned is better than nothing. However, make sure you choose those with no salt added, or that are low in sodium. If this is not an option, rinse them under running water to reduce the salt that is added during the canning process.

Family Meals

Children whose families regularly eat together are less likely to choose unhealthy foods as snack options and are more likely to eat healthy foods like fruits, vegetables, and whole grains. Family meals are likely to be more nutritious than meals where everyone fends for themselves.

Teenagers who regularly eat with their families are less likely to engage in dangerous habits like smoking, drinking, or using drugs. Studies have also found these teens are more likely to continue healthy eating into adulthood. Family dinners also provide the opportunity to catch up on the day-to-day and build meaningful relationships with one another.

Snacks

Snacks are an important part of our daily eating routine. They help fill us up between meals so that we do not overeat at dinnertime. They can also give us a much needed pick-me-up in the middle of the day. Having healthy snack options available can help our families develop better eating habits. Here are some tips:

- Keep fruits and vegetables on hand for quick snacking. Have them washed and cut to make it easy for you and your children. Good ideas are apples, carrot and celery sticks, and bananas.
- Offer vanilla or plain Greek yogurt with fresh berries mixed in. This treat will satisfy your child's sweet tooth and is also healthy!
- Make sure there are a variety of healthy snacks available at your home all the time. A variety of fresh fruits, yogurts, raw vegetables, graham crackers, and peanut butter are good options.
- When buying snacks, remember that reduced-fat does not mean healthier. They may have little nutritious value and contain high amounts of sugar.
- Don't ban sweets and treats. This may cause your child to have an unhealthy attitude. The key is moderation. Let them have occasional treats for a snack, but don't go overboard.
- Don't allow snacking while watching television. This can lead to overeating. Snacks should be eaten at the table, just like meals.

Healthy Beverages

Soft drinks are probably the worst thing children can put into their bodies. Researchers have found that in addition to the added sugar, drinking just one can of soda a day leads to an increase of inattention and aggression in young children. Their recommendation? No soda at all for young children, and even adolescents should imbibe very little.

The best beverage choice for anyone, especially children, is water.

When your child says she is thirsty, offer her water first. Be a role model by drinking water in front of your children. Serve water at meals and snacks, and pack a bottle of water when you are out running errands. To make water more enjoyable for children you can add sliced citrus fruits, cucumbers, or berries for added flavor.

> *Water is the most neglected nutrient in your diet, but one of the most vital.*
>
> —*Julia Child*

Milk is another healthy beverage option. Be sure to buy fat-free or low-fat for children over 2 years old.

Despite what some may say, juice is not always the healthiest beverage choice. Even those that contain 100% juice are full of natural sugars. Juice recommendations for children are as follows (Children's Hunger Alliance):

- 6 months to 3 years: ½ cup (4 ounces) or less per day
- 3 years and older: ¾ cup (6 ounces) or less each day

Strategies for Adding Healthy Foods to Your Family's Diet

While your family becomes accustomed to the habit of healthy eating, you may need to "sneak" healthy foods into their diets. There are a few ways of doing this, and they all take minimal effort:

- Serve one fruit and one vegetable with each meal. Keep in mind the My Plate model: half the plate should be made up of these two food groups.
- If your child's school does not serve healthy lunches, pack your child's lunch. Include healthy options with a sweet fruit for a treat.
- Does your child love ice cream and smoothies? Make your own using frozen fruit, low-fat yogurt, and low-fat milk.
- Finely chop up fresh veggies like carrots and sneak them in your meals. Stir them into spaghetti sauce, quesadillas, soups, pancakes and muffin batter, scrambled eggs, and macaroni and cheese. The kids won't even know they are there!

- Homemade Popsicles. Puree fruits like watermelons, strawberries, or bananas and add water, fruit juice, or yogurt. Place the mixture in a cup in the freezer with a popsicle stick. In a few hours, you will have a fresh fruit snack!
- Add sliced tomato, cucumbers, broccoli, or vegetable juice to your fruit smoothie.
- Use finely diced peas or corn as "sprinkles" on yogurt.

These are just a few "sneaky" ways of getting your child to eat healthier food. Play with these ideas or others and find a way that works for your family. Within a few weeks or months, healthy eating will become second nature.

One important thing to remember when communicating with children is that you should never use food as a reward or punishment. Don't bribe your children to clear their plates or punish them by withholding food. If your child does something wrong don't tell them they won't get any dessert at lunch. Meanwhile, children who are punished for not eating may begin to overeat at other meals because they fear being punished at the next one. If they refuse to eat their green beans, don't bribe them by telling them they will get ice cream if they eat their veggies. These tactics result in poor eating habits.

The Importance of Breakfast

Most mornings are nothing but rush, rush, and rush. It is all you can do to get the kids out the door on time. An easy way to save time may be to skip breakfast, right? This is NOT a good idea. Breakfast is a very important part of the day and can get you and your children off on the right track. Studies have found that kids who eat breakfast are healthier and perform better in school than those who don't eat breakfast. Some good on-the-go ideas for breakfast are yogurt, fruit smoothies, fresh fruit, whole-grain cereal in a bag, and milk or orange juice in a spillproof cup.

> *I wish for your help to create a strong, sustainable movement to educate every child about food, inspire families to cook again and empower people everywhere to fight obesity.*
>
> —*Jamie Oliver*

Meal Planning

Meal planning is hands down the number one way to ensure healthy meals. You can do it once a week, once a month, or as you see fit. Probably the simplest method is to coordinate with your grocery shopping.

When you first begin meal planning you will want to keep in mind your family's lifestyle and regular routine. Do you work part- or full-time? Look at your calendar for special events. Which days are the kids going to be home from school? Make sure you remember to plan for school lunches! Don't forget breakfast ideas too.

Once you've made a list of the meals that must be made in the coming week and the goings-on surrounding them, you can better decide which dishes will be the easiest and healthiest to prepare. Then make a list of all the necessary ingredients before you head to the store. These should include staples you may need like flour and sugar as well as snacks, fresh fruits, and vegetables.

Quick and Healthy Cooking Methods

Steaming: Vegetables, chicken, and shellfish are all delicious when steamed. Steaming seals in the flavor and eliminates the need for fats like butter. All you need is a large pot with a perforated basket that can rest above the water, and a lid. Add water and place food in a single layer in the bottom of the basket. Once the water is boiling, turn the heat off, put the lid on, and allow the boiled water to cook and steam your food for 8 to 10 minutes. For poultry, always use a meat thermometer to test doneness.

Grilling and Broiling: Grilling can be done outdoors on a grill or on a rack set above charcoal embers or gas-heated rocks. Broiling food is done by placing food on a rack below the heating element. Both options cause the fat to drip away from the food—and away from our plates!

Adding Fresh Herbs and Spices: Flavor your food with herbs and spices instead of salt and fat. Fresh herbs should be bright and added toward the end of the cooking process. Dried herbs tend to work best when added during cooking so their flavor has time to infuse the dish. When using dried herbs, use about one-third the amount you would have used of fresh herbs.

Pressure Cooking: Pressure cooking is a great method for the busy home cook and keeps many vitamins and minerals intact. A pressure cooker seals in steam and intensifies the flavor of the food. No need for artificial flavorings, oils, or fats. Soups and stews that may normally take hours to cook can be done in 15 minutes using a pressure cooker. Vegetables and rice can be cooked in 3 to 5 minutes, and a whole chicken can be cooked in as little as 20. When it comes to using a pressure cooker, every second counts, so be sure to use a timer. Also, don't fill your cooker more than two-thirds full. This gives the food room to expand.

Slow Cooking: Slow cookers can be a parent's best friend! If you don't have one, get one that has a timer. This way you can set your cooker to cook on high or low for a designated time. It will automatically turn off and keep your food warm. These are great to use on days you will not be home until dinnertime. Knowing dinner will be ready can be a huge stress reliever and will keep you from heading to the drive-thru.

Eating at Home vs. Eating Out

The *America's Most Wanted Recipes* series is all about eating at home. There are always those days when running through the drive-thru or picking up takeout seems like the easier option. But it's so unhealthy and expensive! Eating at home saves your family money and calories.

According to a recent *New York Times* article, a family of four can eat at McDonald's for $23 to $28. Compare that to a home-cooked meal consisting of a roasted chicken, salad, veggies, and milk, which will cost only $14.

Fast-food meals not only cost more than eating at home, they are also higher in calories and fat. InfoPlease.com shares the following chart that shows the difference between meals at a fast-food restaurant and a meal cooked at home.

The amount of calories and fat saved by eating at home is staggering. Consider this the next time you are contemplating the drive-thru.

There are five fast-food restaurants for every grocery store in the United States. Combine that with the large amount of marketing restau-

FOOD	CALORIES	FAT (GRAMS)
McDonald's Big Mac	563	33
Medium McDonald's french fries	384	20
Medium McDonald's vanilla shake	733	21
Total for one meal	**1,680**	**74**
Burger King Whopper with cheese	790	48
Medium Burger King french fries	387	20
Medium Burger King vanilla shake	667	35
Total for one meal	**1,844**	**103**
Compare those to a meal prepared at home:		
One-half of a roasted chicken breast	142	3
Medium baked white potato	130	0
½ cup green peas 67		0
8-ounce glass of 1% milk	102	3
1 cup unsweetened applesauce	105	0
Total for one meal	**546**	**6**

rants use and there is no wonder that many families choose the route of eating out. Also, the price of fresh produce has increased by 40% over the past decade. In comparison, the price of processed food has decreased by 30%. This leaves many families believing they are unable to afford quality foods for their family. However, there are many ways to lessen the cost of produce and quality food.

Coupons: You don't have to be an extreme couponer. Just clipping a few coupons here and there that you find in the paper or online can save your family money.

Buy foods whole instead of precut: This includes carrots, celery, cheeses, and ground beef. You can separate meat into individual pounds yourself after buying a roll of ground beef. Chopping carrots and celery yourself can save money vs. buying them precut and bagged. Also, you can grate your own cheese and slice it at home after you buy it in a block.

Buy vegetables and fruit in season: This can save a huge amount of money. Figure out what fruits are in season where you live and buy those instead of out-of-season fruits. Items like watermelon are best bought in the summer, apples are cheaper in the fall, and very few fruits are fresh in the winter. These are just a few examples to give you an idea. Just remember to do your research and buy in season only.

When making the transition from eating out to cooking and eating at home you may feel overwhelmed. If your family eats the majority of their meals out now, make the transition slowly. Remember that eating at home just one more day than you do now is better than feeding your family fast food for that evening.

Summary

As parents, it is our job to teach healthy eating habits to our children. It is our job to provide nutritious foods at mealtimes and to make sure they are active and healthy. If we want to turn this country's obesity epidemic around it must start now, and it starts at home.

Remember to plan, to give your children time each day to be active, to have fruits and vegetables available for meals and snacks, and to opt out of the drive-thru lane. As busy parents, we can utilize time-saving tools like pressure cookers, and we can clip coupons and buy in season to save money.

We can provide our families with healthier options, and we can choose to be aware of nutritional content and share that information with our children. We just have to make that choice.

Now let's get cooking!

APPLEBEE'S
Cheesy Bread Pizza

THESE WARM AND CRUNCHY PIZZA BITES ARE SUPER EASY TO PREPARE FOR AN
AFTER-SCHOOL SNACK OR FOR A FULL DINNER WITH SALAD OR MIXED VEGETABLES.

2 tablespoons olive oil
1 (5-inch) loaf French bread, split
  in half lengthwise
2 tablespoons olive oil
½ cup marinara or pizza sauce

½ pound sweet Italian sausage,
  crumbled and cooked
½ cup shredded mozzarella
  cheese

1. Preheat the oven to 375°F. Line a baking sheet with foil.

2. Spread 1 tablespoon of the olive oil over the cut side of each piece of bread. Lay cut side up on the baking sheet and bake until the tops are golden.

3. Meanwhile, in a small saucepan, heat the marinara sauce.

4. When the bread is toasted, spread each piece with the sauce. Follow with the cooked sausage, then sprinkle evenly with the shredded mozzarella. Return to the oven and bake until the cheese melts.

5. Cut each half of bread crosswise into two or three pieces and serve hot.

Makes 2 servings

This recipe can be easily doubled for more servings. This is a great party dish—perfect for a family movie night in. For a little variety, use slices of pepperoni in place of the sausage. You can also go vegetarian using only cheese, chopped tomatoes, and shredded fresh basil.

APPLEBEE'S
Four-Cheese Grille

SLICES OF SHARP AND AGED CHEDDAR ARE GENTLY MELTED WITH ASIAGO AND
PARMESAN CHEESES ON TOASTED RUSTIC BREAD. PERFECT WITH A BOWL OF HOT
SOUP ON A COLD WEEKNIGHT.

4 tablespoons (½ stick) unsalted
butter, softened
8 slices bread, such as Tuscan or
sourdough
4 slices sharp Cheddar cheese

½ cup shredded Asiago cheese
½ cup shredded Parmesan
cheese
4 slices aged white Cheddar
cheese

1. Heat a heavy griddle or large cast-iron skillet over medium-high heat.
2. Evenly spread the butter over both sides of each slice of bread. In the
    skillet, toast all the bread on one side of each slice until golden. Flip 4 of
    the slices over to toast. Reserve the others.
3. Line up the 4 reserved bread slices, toasted side up, and place one slice
    of sharp Cheddar on each. Sprinkle on a layer of Asiago, then Parmesan.
    Finish with a slice of the aged white Cheddar.
4. Top each sandwich with the fully toasted bread slices. Place each sand-
    wich in the skillet, untoasted side down. When the bread is golden and
    the cheese melted, cut each sandwich in half and serve while still warm.

Makes 4 servings

*To keep the cheese from melting onto the griddle, you may need to cut
the sliced pieces in half and shingle them over the bread. Other cheeses
can be used, such as Swiss, mozzarella, Monterey Jack, or American
cheese. Look for reduced- or low-fat varieties to save a few calories.*

APPLEBEE'S
Kids' Mini Hamburgers

THESE MINI BURGERS ARE SIMILAR TO APPLEBEE'S SLIDERS FOR GROWN-UPS. PLAN ON MAKING TWO BURGERS PER SERVING FOR KIDS AND ADD A SLICE OF CHEDDAR OR SWISS CHEESE FOR AN EXTRA TREAT. FOR SOPHISTICATED TASTES, ADD APPLEBEE'S SIGNATURE SLIDER SAUCE.

1 pound lean ground sirloin or chuck
½ teaspoon onion powder
½ teaspoon garlic powder
1 teaspoon kosher salt
½ teaspoon pepper

8 slices cheese, for cheeseburgers (optional)
8 (3-inch) mini hamburger buns, split in half
Applebee's Slider Sauce (optional; recipe follows)

1. In a bowl, mix the ground beef, onion powder, garlic powder, salt, and pepper. Divide the meat into 8 even portions and gently roll into balls. Lightly flatten the balls into patties.

2. Preheat the broiler.

3. Heat a griddle or skillet over medium-high heat. Cook each patty for 2 to 3 minutes per side, or until cooked to your desired doneness. (If making cheeseburgers, add a slice of cheese when you flip patties over after cooking one side, and let it melt slightly.)

4. While the burgers are cooking, put the buns on a baking sheet or broiler pan and toast them lightly under the broiler until they are golden.

5. To assemble the sliders, put one patty on each bottom bun and finish with the top bun. If serving slider sauce, after toasting the hamburger buns, spread about 1 teaspoon on the toasted side of both the top and bottom buns before assembling each slider.

Makes 4 servings

Applebee's Slider Sauce

¼ cup mayonnaise
¼ cup Dijon mustard
¼ cup honey

1 tablespoon dry mustard
1 tablespoon apple cider vinegar
¼ teaspoon smoked paprika

Whisk together all the ingredients and keep refrigerated in a tightly sealed container until ready to use.

Makes about ¾ cup

APPLEBEE'S
Peanut Butter Cup Cheesecake

THOUGH NO LONGER ON THE APPLEBEE'S DESSERT MENU, THIS CREAMY PIE IS STILL A FAVORITE IN MANY CHOCOLATE AND PEANUT BUTTER LOVERS' HEARTS. USE MINI PEANUT BUTTER CUPS FOR EASIER CHOPPING.

2 cups chocolate cookies
1 cup peanut butter cookies
8 tablespoons (1 stick) unsalted butter, melted
1¾ cups light brown sugar
4 (8-ounce) packages cream cheese, softened
½ cup creamy peanut butter

4 eggs
1½ teaspoons vanilla extract
1 cup sour cream
2 cups peanut butter cups, chopped
½ cup heavy (whipping) cream
1¼ cups finely chopped milk chocolate

1. Position a rack in the center of the oven and preheat to 325°F. Line the outside bottom and sides of a 9-inch springform pan with foil.

2. In a food processor, combine the chocolate and peanut butter cookies and pulse until they are ground into crumbs. Add the melted butter and ¼ cup of the brown sugar and pulse until well mixed.

3. Press the crumb mixture firmly over the bottom and halfway up the sides of the prepared pan and set it aside.

4. In a bowl, with an electric mixer on low speed, beat the cream cheese, peanut butter, and remaining 1½ cups brown sugar until smooth and creamy. Add the eggs, one at a time, beating well after each addition, then stir in the vanilla and sour cream. Fold in the chopped peanut butter cups.

5. Put the springform pan into a larger roasting pan. Pour the batter into the cookie crust. Fill the larger pan with warm water, so that it reaches halfway up the sides of the springform pan.

6. Bake for 50 minutes. Turn off the heat and leave the cake in the oven for 1 hour without opening the door.

7. Remove the cake from the oven and let it cool completely. Cover it and refrigerate for at least 4 hours, or preferably overnight.

8. In a small saucepan, heat the cream just to a simmer. Stir in the milk chocolate, remove the pan from the heat, and stir until the chocolate is melted and the mixture is smooth.

9. Remove the ring from around the chilled cake and spoon the chocolate icing over the top and sides. Let it firm up in the refrigerator before slicing.

Makes 8 to 12 servings

For a special occasion, chop additional peanut butter cups and milk chocolate to sprinkle over the finished cake.

APPLEBEE'S
Southern Chicken Sliders

- -

MAKE EVERYONE HAPPY, NOT JUST THE KIDS, WITH THESE CHICKEN TENDERS
COATED IN GENTLE SPICES THEN FRIED UNTIL CRUNCHY AND GOLDEN. SERVE
THEM WITH APPLEBEE'S SIGNATURE HONEY MUSTARD SAUCE ALONG WITH CRISP
DILL PICKLES.

- -

1 egg
1 cup buttermilk
1 pound chicken tenders, cut into
    1-inch strips
1 cup all-purpose flour
1 cup seasoned bread crumbs,
    store-bought or homemade
1½ teaspoons granulated garlic

1 teaspoon baking powder
1 teaspoon kosher salt
½ teaspoon pepper
3 to 4 cups vegetable oil
Honey Mustard Sauce (recipe
    follows)
8 (3-inch) mini hamburger buns,
    split and toasted

1. In a medium bowl, beat the egg well. Whisk in the buttermilk. Add the
   chicken strips, and toss to coat thoroughly. Refrigerate, covered, for at
   least 1 hour.

2. In a medium bowl, combine the flour, bread crumbs, granulated garlic,
   baking powder, salt, and pepper. Whisk the ingredients until they are
   completely mixed. Transfer to a resealable plastic bag.

3. In a medium saucepan or deep skillet, heat the oil over medium-high
   heat.

4. Shake the excess buttermilk off each piece of chicken and coat them in
   the breading by tossing a few pieces at a time in the plastic bag. When all
   the pieces have been coated, fry them in batches in the hot oil, turning
   once after the bottom sides are golden brown.

5. Drain the chicken on paper towels to absorb excess oil.

6. Spread 1 teaspoon of the honey mustard sauce on the bottom half of each bun. (Or you may serve the sauce on the side.) Layer with 2 or 3 pieces of the fried chicken, then finish with the top bun. Any extra pieces of fried chicken can be served separately.

Makes 4 servings

Be sure to serve these sliders with a tray of your favorite accompaniments, such as tomato slices, crisp lettuce, and thin slices of red onion. A sprinkling of Parmesan cheese on the hot chicken adds extra flavor.

Honey Mustard Sauce

¼ cup mayonnaise, regular or
low-fat

¼ cup Dijon mustard

¼ cup honey

1 tablespoon dry mustard

1 tablespoon apple cider vinegar

¼ teaspoon paprika

Whisk together all the ingredients and keep refrigerated in a tightly sealed container until ready to use.

Makes about ¾ cup

ARBY'S

Curly Fries

ARBY'S HAS HAD SUCH GREAT SUCCESS WITH THEIR CURLY FRIES THAT THEY
STARTED SELLING THEM PACKAGED AND READY TO BE BAKED AT HOME. IF YOU
DON'T ALREADY HAVE A CURLY FRY CUTTER, TRY USING BAMBOO SKEWERS AND A
SHARP KNIFE (SEE STEP 2).

½ cup all-purpose flour
1½ teaspoons kosher salt
3 tablespoons cornstarch
1 teaspoon onion powder
½ teaspoon granulated garlic

2 teaspoons paprika
2 teaspoons baking soda
2 pounds small russet potatoes
3 to 4 cups vegetable oil

1. In a bowl, whisk together the flour, salt, cornstarch, onion powder,
   granulated garlic, paprika, and baking soda.

2. Cut a small slice off one end of a potato and set the potato upright on
   the cut end. Center a 6-inch skewer into the potato from the top and
   gently push it through until it hits your cutting board. Lay the potato on
   its side and, using a thin-bladed knife, turn the potato counter-clockwise
   as you slice the potato all the way to the skewer, pulling the knife clock-
   wise to thinly slice it.

3. When you have sliced through the whole potato from end to end, gently
   fan it out so that the individual slices are exposed, covering most of the
   length of the skewer. Leave the potatoes on the skewers.

4. In a large, heavy-bottomed saucepan or deep skillet, heat the vegetable
   oil to between 350° and 375°F using a deep-fry/candy thermometer or
   instant-read thermometer to determine the temperature.

5. Coat the potatoes thoroughly with the flour mixture and fry them in the
   hot oil, a couple of skewers at a time, until they are golden brown. Turn
   them often to make sure each side is frying evenly.

6. Drain the skewers on paper towels. When the potatoes have cooled a bit, gently slide them off the skewers and serve with your favorite condiments.

Makes 3 or 4 servings

A curly fry cutter can be found online and at large retailers, and generally starts in the $100 price range. It can also be used on apples, zucchini, and daikon radishes. A great way to create garnishes.

ARBY'S
Jr Bacon Cheddar Melt

THIS SANDWICH CAN GO FROM LEFTOVERS TO LUNCH SACK IN JUST MINUTES. IT'S A GREAT USE OF LEFTOVER SLICES OF ARBY'S ROAST BEEF, A DELI PURCHASE, OR YOUR OWN JUICY POT ROAST.

4 slices bacon
2 tablespoons coarsely ground black pepper
4 ounces cooked roast beef, thinly sliced

2 sesame seed hamburger buns, split in half and toasted
¼ cup melted Cheddar cheese, heated

1. Sprinkle each side of the bacon with pepper. Heat a large skillet over medium-high heat and cook the peppered bacon until crispy. Drain on paper towels.

2. Heat the roast beef in a microwave or wipe the pepper from the skillet and heat the roast beef with a small amount of water or beef broth.

3. Pile the beef on the bottom of each toasted bun and top with two slices of the peppered bacon. Spoon a portion of the melted Cheddar over the bacon and top the sandwiches with the remaining half bun.

Makes 2 servings

A toaster oven or a hot broiler can melt a slice of Cheddar, American, or Swiss cheese. You can also use Velveeta or a prepared cheese sauce.

ARBY'S
Jr Turkey & Cheese Sandwich

KIDS WILL LOVE THE TASTE OF THINLY SLICED TURKEY WITH SHARP CHEDDAR CHEESE. TOAST THE SESAME SEED BUNS AND SERVE THE SANDWICHES PLAIN, OR WITH LETTUCE, TOMATO, AND SLICED RED ONION.

4 ounces roasted turkey breast, thinly sliced

2 sesame seed hamburger buns, split in half and toasted
2 slices sharp Cheddar cheese

1. Heat the sliced turkey in a microwave or in a skillet with a small amount of water.
2. Pile the turkey on the bottom bun, top with the Cheddar cheese, and finish with the remaining half bun.

Makes 2 servings

A quick sauce of mayonnaise, sweet pickle relish, and a dash of ketchup makes a tasty spread for the bottom of the bun, if desired.

AUNTIE ANNE'S
Cinnamon Sugar Pretzel Bites

AUNTIE ANNE'S STARTED IN PENNSYLVANIA MAKING BASIC PRETZELS AND IS NOW
A NATIONAL CHAIN WITH BOTH SWEET AND SAVORY TEMPTATIONS FOR SALE.
THESE TENDER BITES TAKE A WHILE TO ASSEMBLE, BUT THE RESULTS ARE WELL
WORTH THE EFFORT. SERVE THEM WITH CREAM CHEESE DIPPING SAUCE (RECIPE
FOLLOWS).

Pretzel Bites

1 cup warm water

1 envelope active dry yeast
   (2¼ teaspoons)

3 tablespoons granulated sugar

2 tablespoons light brown sugar

1 tablespoon vegetable oil

1 teaspoon kosher salt

1½ cups bread flour

1 cup all-purpose flour, plus more
   as needed

3 cups hot water

¼ cup baking soda

Cinnamon Sugar Coating

½ cup granulated sugar

1 tablespoon ground cinnamon

8 tablespoons (1 stick) unsalted
   butter, melted

1. **Make the pretzel bites:** In a stand mixer, combine the warm water,
   yeast, and ½ teaspoon granulated sugar and stir to dissolve the sugar. Let
   the mixture stand about 10 minutes.

2. Whisk in the remaining 2 tablespoons plus 2 teaspoons granulated sugar,
   the brown sugar, vegetable oil, and salt. With the paddle attachment,
   slowly add the bread flour on low speed and mix until well blended.
   (Alternatively, do this with a hand-mixer.)

3. Switch to a dough hook and slowly mix in the all-purpose flour. (Stir in
   the flour with a wooden spoon if not using a stand mixer.)

4. Knead the mixture until smooth and elastic, adding a little more all-
   purpose flour if needed to make a soft and slightly sticky dough.

5. Lightly oil a large glass or metal bowl. Transfer the kneaded dough to the bowl, cover with plastic wrap, and let it rise in a draft-free area until doubled in size, about 1½ hours.

6. Preheat the oven to 425°F. Line 2 baking sheets with silicone baking mats.

7. Punch the dough down and divide it into 6 equal portions. Work with one piece at a time and keep the remaining pieces covered with the plastic wrap to keep from drying out. Roll each portion of the dough into a long rope about 2 feet long. Using a ruler for accuracy, cut each rope into bite-size pieces 1¼ inches long.

8. In a bowl, whisk together the hot water and baking soda, stirring until the soda is dissolved. Dip several pretzel pieces into the solution, then lift them out with a slotted spoon or wire strainer. Let the extra moisture drip off, then transfer them to the lined baking sheets, arranging them in a single layer.

9. Bake the pretzels for 8 to 11 minutes, or until the tops are golden brown.

10. **Make the cinnamon sugar coating:** In a small bowl, whisk together the granulated sugar and cinnamon.

11. Dip the baked pieces into the melted butter, coating them evenly. Let them rest a minute or two on a plate, then roll each pretzel in the coating mix. Let sit a minute before serving warm with the cream cheese dipping sauce.

Makes 10 servings

If this recipe takes more time than you have, you'll still be able to put smiles on little faces by using the Auntie Anne's Pretzels & More Homemade Baking Mix available at selected retail stores. With the basic pretzel dough, you can create your own recipes for desserts or snacks.

Cream Cheese Dipping Sauce

4 ounces cream cheese, softened

2 tablespoons unsalted butter, softened

1 cup powdered sugar

½ teaspoon vanilla extract

2 tablespoons heavy (whipping) cream

1. In a bowl, with an electric mixer, whip the cream cheese and butter until smooth and creamy. Beat in the powdered sugar and vanilla.

2. In a separate bowl, whip the cream until stiff peaks form, then fold into the cream cheese and butter mixture. Refrigerate covered until ready to serve.

AUNTIE ANNE'S
Mini Pretzel Dogs

KIDS AND GROWN-UPS ALIKE WILL LOVE THESE SAVORY BITES OF PRETZEL AND MINI-SAUSAGE. IF YOU CAN'T FIND THE AUNTIE ANNE'S BAKING MIX, USE THE PRETZEL DOUGH RECIPE FROM THE CINNAMON SUGAR PRETZEL BITES RECIPE (PAGE 37).

1 box Auntie Anne's Pretzels & More Homemade Baking Mix
2 (14-ounce) packages Lit'l Smokies or other cocktail sausages
Cooking spray
4 cups hot water
¼ cup baking soda
4 tablespoons (½ stick) unsalted butter (optional)

1. Prepare the pretzel dough according to package directions.

2. Drain the Smokies on paper towels and set aside.

3. Position a rack in the center of the oven and preheat to 350°F. Lightly coat one or two baking sheets with cooking spray.

4. Spray a work surface with the cooking spray and turn the risen dough out onto that surface. Divide the dough into 8 portions and pat each into a piece about 4½ inches long by 1½ inches wide. Roll or stretch each piece into a rope 27 inches long by ⅜ inch wide.

5. Starting at one end of a rope, lay a sausage perpendicular to the dough. Wrap the dough once around the center of the sausage and pull the dough apart from the rest of the rope. Set the wrapped Lit'l Smokie seam side down on a baking sheet. Continue with the rest of the sausages and ropes of dough. You should have about 80 pieces when finished.

6. In a bowl, whisk together the hot water and baking soda, stirring until the soda is dissolved. Dip each pretzel dog into the solution and return to the baking sheet, shaking off excess liquid.

7. Bake one sheet at a time for 12 to 15 minutes, or until each pretzel dog is golden brown. Since oven calibrations may vary, be sure to rotate the baking sheet front to back halfway through the baking time.

8. Melt the butter (if using) and brush each mini dog over the top while still warm to give the pretzel dough a shiny finish.

Makes 80 pieces

Lit'l Smokies are a mix of turkey and pork and are lower in fat than an all-pork sausage. You may find other cocktail sausages to use for variety, and can mix them up when making this recipe for a crowd.

BASKIN-ROBBINS
Peanut Butter 'n Chocolate Ice Cream

- -

YOU'LL NEED AN ICE CREAM MAKER FOR THIS RECIPE, BUT THE HAPPY SMILES ON
DELIGHTED FACES WILL MAKE IT ALL WORTH IT.

- -

2½ cups milk

1 cup sugar

⅓ cup unsweetened dark cocoa
 powder

¼ teaspoon kosher salt

3 tablespoons cornstarch

½ cup heavy (whipping) cream

¾ cup bittersweet chocolate
 chips

⅓ cup creamy peanut butter

1. In a medium saucepan, combine 2 cups of the milk, the sugar, cocoa
   powder, and salt. Place it over medium heat and bring it almost to a boil.

2. In a bowl, combine the remaining ½ cup milk and the cornstarch,
   whisking until there are no lumps.

3. Whisk the cornstarch mixture into the hot milk and bring it to a low
   boil over medium-low heat. Let simmer until thickened to the consistency of pudding, then remove from the heat.

4. In a small saucepan, bring the heavy cream to a low boil. Place the
   chocolate chips in a heatproof bowl and pour the hot cream over them.
   Stir the chips until they are completely melted.

5. Stir the melted chip mixture into the chocolate pudding and whisk until
   well combined.

6. Pour the ice cream base into a bowl, cover with plastic, and refrigerate
   for at least 4 hours or overnight.

7. Pour the chilled base into an ice cream maker and process according to
   the manufacturer's directions. Once the ice cream is thickened, and with
   the motor of the machine running, drop small spoonfuls of the peanut
   butter into the machine. If you do this right before the ice cream is

finished, you will get lovely ribbons of peanut butter swirled throughout the ice cream.

8. Transfer the finished ice cream to a freezer container with a tight lid and freeze until needed.

* * * * * * * * *

Makes 6 to 8 servings

* * * * * * * * *

A lighter chocolate ice cream can be made using regular or light cocoa powder and milk chocolate or white chocolate chips.

BEN & JERRY'S
Chunky Monkey Ice Cream

BEN & JERRY'S IS KNOWN FOR ITS CREATIVE ICE CREAM FLAVOR NAMES. SEE IF YOU CAN COME UP WITH AN EVEN WACKIER ONE FOR THIS DECADENT BLEND OF CHOCOLATE, NUTS, BANANAS, AND THICK AND LUSCIOUS CREAM!

4.5 ounces solid dark chocolate, chopped into chunks
2 egg yolks
¾ cup sugar
2 cups heavy (whipping) cream
1 cup milk

2 teaspoons vanilla extract
2 overripe bananas, mashed until smooth
Juice of 1 lemon
½ cup chopped walnuts (optional)

1. Put the chopped chocolate in a bowl, cover the bowl, and refrigerate it.

2. In a medium bowl, with an electric mixer, beat the eggs and sugar until light and fluffy. Beat in the heavy cream and milk until well blended. Stir in the vanilla.

3. Pour the mixture into a saucepan and place over low heat. Stir frequently until the mixture thickens slightly and coats the back of a spoon and reaches 170° to 175°F. Turn the stove off and let the mixture cool slightly.

4. Transfer the mixture to an ice cream maker and process according to the manufacturer's directions. Just before the ice cream is done, after it has thickened, add the mashed banana, lemon juice, chilled chunks of chocolate, and the walnuts (if using).

5. Transfer the ice cream to a freezer container with a tight lid and freeze until needed.

Makes 6 to 8 servings

Add ¼ cup of creamy peanut butter in place of 1 of the bananas to make an even happier chunky monkey!

BEN & JERRY'S
Orange Cream Dream Ice Cream

THE NAME OF THIS SMOOTH TEMPTATION IS KIND OF PSYCHEDELIC, BUT THERE'S NOTHING FUZZY ABOUT THE YUMMINESS OF THIS RECIPE. BE SURE TO USE GENUINE VANILLA EXTRACT FOR DEPTH AND FLAVOR.

¾ cup sugar

2 eggs

2 cups heavy (whipping) cream

I cup milk

2 teaspoons vanilla extract

⅓ cup frozen orange juice concentrate, thawed

1. In a medium bowl, with an electric mixer, beat the sugar and eggs until light and fluffy. Beat in the heavy cream and milk until well blended. Stir in the vanilla and orange juice concentrate and mix well.

2. Pour the mixture into a saucepan and place over low heat. Stir frequently until the mixture thickens slightly and coats the back of a spoon and reaches 170° to 175°F. Turn the stove off and let the mixture cool slightly.

3. Pour the mixture into an ice cream maker and process according to the manufacturer's directions.

4. Transfer the finished ice cream to a freezer container with a tight lid and freeze until needed.

Makes 6 to 8 servings

Once you get this recipe down, try making it with tangerine or grapefruit juice for a tangy twist.

BENIHANA

Seafood Tempura

THE PERFECT WAY TO SNEAK VEGGIES INTO YOUR KIDS' BELLIES! THIS RECIPE PROVIDES A BASIC BUT TERRIFIC TEMPURA BATTER THAT CAN BE USED TO COAT SEAFOOD AS WELL. BE SURE YOUR OIL IS BETWEEN 375° AND 400°F, AND MAINTAIN THAT TEMPERATURE WHILE FRYING ITEMS IN BATCHES. A DEEP-FRY/CANDY THERMOMETER WILL HELP YOU WITH THIS.

2 eggs

1 cup ice water

2 cups rice flour

1 quart canola or peanut oil

8 medium shiitake mushrooms, stemmed, an "X" cut into each cap

1 carrot, peeled, halved crosswise, and cut lengthwise into 1/16-inch-thick strips

1 medium waxy potato, such as White Rose, thinly sliced

1 green bell pepper, cut into 1/4-inch-wide strips

1 pound calamari, cleaned, sliced, dried, and chilled

6 medium sea scallops

8 large shrimp, peeled and deveined

1. In a bowl, beat the eggs well. Stir in the ice water, then add the rice flour all at once. Mix the batter until it is combined but not overly mixed. The batter will be too heavy if it is blended too thoroughly.

2. In a wok or large saucepan, heat the oil to 350°F. When the oil is very hot, coat a few vegetables at a time in the batter, removing excess, and fry on both sides until puffy. Drain on paper towels or a wire rack.

3. Bring the oil back to temperature and batter and fry the seafood, starting with the calamari, then scallops, then the shrimp.

4. Serve the tempura while still warm with your favorite dipping sauce.

Makes 4 servings

Unlike most batters that brown during the frying process, tempura batter stays a fairly pale white. While cooking, you may need to remove stray pieces of batter from the oil to prevent them from burning and flavoring the oil. You can do this while waiting for the oil to return to the proper temperature.

BENNIGAN'S
Meatloaf

THE BENNIGAN'S STORY IS AN EXAMPLE OF TREMENDOUS WILL OVER IMPRESSIVE ODDS. ONCE BANKRUPT AND ALMOST FORGOTTEN, THE CHAIN HAS BEEN RENEWED AND INVIGORATED AND CONTINUES TO GROW. ALTHOUGH SEVERAL FAVORITE MENU ITEMS WERE DROPPED, SOME FRANCHISES STILL OFFER THE MEATLOAF FROM THE ORIGINAL CONCEPT. BETTER TO TRY THIS FAMILY-PLEASING VERSION AT HOME!

Cooking spray or vegetable oil
3 pounds lean ground beef
1 pound bulk sweet Italian sausage
4 large yellow onions, chopped
1 large green bell pepper
½ cup tomato paste
3 eggs, well beaten

2 teaspoons Worcestershire sauce
1 tablespoon granulated garlic
1 tablespoon dried minced onion
1 teaspoon black pepper
1 cup grated Parmesan cheese
½ cup tomato sauce
½ cup packed light brown sugar

1. Preheat the oven to 350°F. Coat a 9 x 5-inch loaf pan with cooking spray or vegetable oil.

2. In a large bowl, combine the ground beef, sausage, onions, bell pepper, tomato paste, eggs, Worcestershire sauce, garlic, dried onion, black pepper, and Parmesan. Mix the ingredients with your hands, or use the beater attachment of a stand mixer to thoroughly blend all the ingredients.

3. Pack the meat mixture into the loaf pan. Rap the filled pan a couple of times on a counter or sturdy table to settle the mixture.

4. In a small bowl, whisk together the tomato sauce and brown sugar. Spoon the mixture over the meatloaf and cover the pan with foil.

5. Bake for 1 hour. Remove the foil and continue to bake until the top is browned, about 30 minutes. Let cool completely before removing the loaf from the pan.

Makes 8 to 10 servings

Mashed potatoes with peas and carrots will round this out to make a perfect dinner plate. Use some of the drippings from the finished meatloaf to make your own gravy.

BERTUCCI'S
Chicken Piccata

MAKE REGULAR OLD CHICKEN SPECIAL WITH THIS CLASSIC ITALIAN RECIPE. EVEN THE PICKIEST PALATES WILL LOVE THE CONTRASTING FLAVORS OF BUTTER AND CAPERS.

4 boneless, skinless chicken breasts
Kosher salt and pepper
½ cup all-purpose flour
¼ cup vegetable oil
½ cup dry white wine or chicken broth

4 tablespoons (½ stick) unsalted butter
¼ cup capers, rinsed
3 tablespoons lemon juice
¼ cup chopped parsley

1. Place each chicken breast between two sheets of plastic wrap and pound it with a meat mallet until evenly thinned to about ¼ inch.

2. Season the chicken with salt and pepper. Dust flour on both sides.

3. In a large skillet, heat the oil. Working in batches if necessary, add the chicken and cook until lightly browned on each side. Remove the cooked chicken and keep warm.

4. For the delicious sauce, drain all but 1 tablespoon of the oil from the skillet. Pour in the wine or broth and cook over medium heat, scraping up any browned bits. Whisk in the butter, capers, and lemon juice. Let the sauce cook for 2 to 3 minutes. Stir in half the chopped parsley.

5. Spoon the sauce over the chicken breasts and sprinkle with the remaining parsley. Serve warm.

Makes 4 servings

Mashed potatoes and a fresh vegetable, such as steamed carrots or broccoli, will make a quick and easy midweek dinner.

BERTUCCI'S
Four-Cheese Ravioli

UNLESS YOU ARE VERY HANDY WITH PASTA DOUGH, I RECOMMEND YOU PURCHASE FRESH OR FROZEN RAVIOLI. LOOK FOR A FOUR-CHEESE VARIETY AND COOK ACCORDING TO THE PACKAGE DIRECTIONS.

2 tablespoons olive oil

4 tablespoons (½ stick) unsalted butter

2 cloves garlic, minced

½ pound cremini mushrooms, stemmed and sliced

5 ounces shiitake mushrooms, stemmed and sliced

½ cup dry white wine or chicken broth

½ teaspoon kosher salt

¼ teaspoon pepper

½ cup Italian parsley, leaves only, chopped

1 pound four-cheese ravioli, cooked

1. In a large skillet, heat the olive oil and 2 tablespoons of the butter over medium heat. Add the garlic and cook until softened.

2. Stir in the cremini and shiitake mushrooms and cook, stirring frequently, until their liquid has been released and evaporated. The mushrooms should be lightly golden brown.

3. Add the wine or chicken broth and bring to a boil. Let the liquid evaporate, then season with the salt, pepper, and 1 tablespoon parsley.

4. Stir in the remaining 2 tablespoons butter. When it has melted, add the cooked ravioli and gently stir to coat them with the mushrooms.

5. Sprinkle with the remaining parsley and serve warm.

Makes 4 to 6 servings

For even more delicious cheese, pass some grated Parmesan around the table to finish the dish.

BOB EVANS
Cheddar Baked Potato Soup

THIS SOUP IS RICHLY FLAVORED WITH CHEDDAR CHEESE, MILK, AND POTATOES. SURE TO FILL UP HUNGRY BELLIES FAST, IT'S VIRTUALLY A MEAL ON ITS OWN. A FRESH SALAD ON THE SIDE IS A REFRESHING ACCOMPANIMENT.

7 cups peeled and cubed (1-inch) russet (baking) potatoes

1 (10.75-ounce) can condensed Cheddar cheese soup, like Campbell's

1¼ cups chicken broth

5¼ cups milk

2 cups shredded Cheddar cheese

2 tablespoons cornstarch

2 tablespoons unsalted butter

½ teaspoon kosher salt

½ teaspoon pepper

½ teaspoon dried minced onion

½ teaspoon granulated garlic

1. Boil or microwave the diced potatoes until cooked through but still firm. Set them aside.

2. In a large saucepan, stir together the soup, half of the chicken broth, and 1¼ cups of the milk until blended. Bring to a low boil and stir in the Cheddar and remaining 4 cups milk. Stir frequently until the cheese is melted.

3. In a small bowl, whisk together the remaining chicken broth and the cornstarch. Whisk the mixture into the simmering soup and cook until the soup has thickened.

4. Reduce the heat and stir in the potatoes, butter, salt, pepper, dried onion, and garlic and simmer for 15 minutes, or until the potatoes are heated through.

Makes 6 to 8 servings

For a fuller flavor, refrigerate the soup overnight and gently reheat it the next day.

BOB EVANS

Multigrain Blueberry Hotcakes

THESE ARE HEARTY, FILLING PANCAKES. THE WHOLE WHEAT PASTRY FLOUR GIVES
THEM A DENSE, CHEWY QUALITY. WHAT THEY LACK IN FLUFFINESS IS MADE UP FOR
HEALTH-WISE, AS WHOLE WHEAT FLOUR IS FAR MORE NUTRITIOUS THAN WHITE.
USE YOUR LEFTOVER FLOUR FOR HEALTHY WAFFLES, BISCUITS, AND PIZZA DOUGH.

1½ cups whole wheat pastry
   flour
½ cup quick-cooking oats
½ teaspoon baking powder
½ teaspoon baking soda
1¾ cups milk, whole or 2%
1 egg, separated

2 tablespoons light brown sugar
1 tablespoon vegetable oil
1 cup blueberries, fresh or
   thawed frozen
2 to 3 tablespoons unsalted
   butter, melted

1. In a bowl, whisk together the flour, oats, baking powder, and baking soda.

2. In a separate bowl, whisk together the milk, egg yolk, brown sugar, and
   vegetable oil. Stir the milk mixture into the flour and stir until well
   blended. Fold in the blueberries and stir until just mixed.

3. In a small bowl, with an electric mixer, beat the egg white until it holds
   soft peaks. Fold the egg white into the hotcake batter and set aside for a
   few minutes.

4. Heat a large griddle or skillet over medium heat. Coat lightly with a little
   melted butter and pour ½ cup of batter onto the skillet for each hotcake.
   Flip each cake over when it bubbles through the batter on top and the
   bottom is golden brown. This batter will make about a dozen pancakes,
   although your number may vary somewhat.

Makes 4 to 6 servings

*Use this recipe for waffles! Substitute 2 beaten egg whites for the
whole egg and follow the rest of the directions. Lightly coat a
waffle iron with the melted butter, pour ½ cup batter into the
hot iron, and bake until golden on both sides.*

BONEFISH GRILL
Corn Chowder with Lump Crab

JUICY AND SWEET LUMP CRABMEAT IS AVAILABLE REFRIGERATED, IN CANS, OR FROZEN, IF FRESH CRABMEAT IS NOT AVAILABLE IN THE SEAFOOD SECTION OF YOUR LOCAL MARKET. YOU MAY FIND DUNGENESS OR ALASKAN KING CRAB AVAILABLE AT CERTAIN TIMES OF THE YEAR, AND BY ALL MEANS USE FRESH CRAB WHEN IT'S AVAILABLE.

1 russet (baking) potato, peeled and cubed
5 slices smoked bacon, chopped
½ cup chopped yellow onion
6 ounces lump crabmeat
½ teaspoon dried parsley
2 tablespoons unsalted butter
¼ cup all-purpose flour
¼ cup dry white wine or vermouth

1 cube chicken bouillon
1½ cups whole milk, plus more if needed
1 (15-ounce) can cream-style corn
1 teaspoon kosher salt
¼ teaspoon pepper
Snipped fresh chives or chopped dill, for garnish (optional)

1. Put the potato cubes in a microwave-safe dish, cover it with vented plastic wrap, and microwave for 1 minute. Set aside.

2. In a large skillet, cook the bacon for 2 minutes, stirring occasionally. Add the onion and cook until softened. Remove from heat and stir in the crabmeat and dried parsley.

3. In a large saucepan or soup pot, melt the butter over medium-low heat and whisk in the flour. Stir the mixture until the flour takes on a light tan color. Whisk in the wine or vermouth and stir until the mixture absorbs the liquid.

4. Crumble the bouillon cube into the milk, then slowly whisk that into the simmering flour mixture. When the thickened milk/flour mixture is creamy, stir in the bacon/crab mixture, potatoes, and creamed corn. Thin out the soup with a little more milk if it is too thick for your taste.

5. Season the soup with the salt and pepper and let it simmer for about 10 minutes.

6. Serve garnished with chives or dill, if desired.

Makes 3 servings

Fresh corn is abundant during the summer months. Take advantage of the seasonal availability and use 2 cups freshly shucked corn kernels instead of canned for your chowder!

BOSTON MARKET
Cornbread

. . . .

IF YOUR LOCAL GROCER DOESN'T CARRY THE BOSTON MARKET CORNBREAD MIX,
THIS RECIPE IS AN EXCELLENT FACSIMILE. CHALLENGE YOUR KIDS TO A TASTING
CONTEST USING THE ORIGINAL. I BET THEY WON'T KNOW THE DIFFERENCE!

. . . .

Shortening or cooking spray, for
   the pan
2 (8.5-ounce) boxes cornbread
   mix, such as Jiffy
1 (18.5-ounce) box yellow cake
   mix

¼ teaspoon kosher salt
5 eggs
⅔ cup milk
1 cup water
½ cup canola oil

1. Preheat the oven to 350°F. Lightly coat a 9 x 13-inch baking dish with
   shortening or cooking spray.

2. In a bowl, whisk together the cornbread mix, cake mix, and salt.

3. In a separate bowl, beat the eggs well, then stir in the milk, water, and
   oil. Stir the egg mixture into the dry ingredients and mix just until
   blended.

4. Pour the batter into the baking dish and bake for 25 to 30 minutes, or
   until a toothpick inserted in the center comes out clean.

5. Let the cornbread sit for about 5 minutes before cutting into squares.

Makes 15 to 18 servings

Stale cornbread can be saved and crumbled for use in stuffing,
or cubed and used in trifled desserts!

BOSTON MARKET
Rotisserie Chicken

REMEMBER WHEN BOSTON MARKET WAS KNOWN AS BOSTON CHICKEN? THIS IS
THE RECIPE THAT PUT THE RESTAURANT CHAIN ON THE MAP.

½ cup olive or canola oil
¼ cup apple cider vinegar
2 tablespoons light brown sugar
2 tablespoons minced garlic

2 tablespoons kosher salt
1 whole roasting chicken
(3½ to 4 pounds)

1. In a small bowl, whisk together the oil, vinegar, and sugar until the sugar dissolves. Stir in the garlic and salt.

2. Put the chicken in a large glass or plastic container and pour the marinade over it. Turn the chicken several times so that it is completely coated. Cover the container and refrigerate the chicken overnight. Turn the chicken once or twice during the marinating time.

3. Remove it from the refrigerator about 20 minutes before cooking.

4. Preheat the oven to 350°F.

5. Shake off any excess marinade and roast the chicken breast side up, for about 1 hour, or until an instant-read thermometer inserted in the thickest part of the thigh reaches 160°F.

6. Let the chicken rest about 15 minutes before carving and serving.

Makes 4 to 6 servings

Serve with your favorite sides, such as steamed vegetables or coleslaw. This is a perfect dish to serve with the Boston Market Cornbread (page 54).

BUBBA GUMP SHRIMP CO.

Shrimp Mac and Cheese

BUBBA GUMP MAKES THIS MOUTHWATERING THREE-CHEESE CASSEROLE THAT CAN EASILY BE SERVED AS A SIDE DISH OR ENTRÉE. SKIP THE SHRIMP FOR VEGETARIANS AND PICKY EATERS.

1 pound medium shrimp, peeled and deveined

8 tablespoons (1 stick) unsalted butter

1 teaspoon Cajun seasoning, store-bought or homemade

1 tablespoon dried minced onion

3 tablespoons all-purpose flour

3 cups milk

8 ounces Cheddar cheese, shredded

16 ounces Monterey Jack cheese, shredded

1 teaspoon kosher salt

¼ teaspoon pepper

1 pound elbow macaroni, cooked according to package directions

½ cup unseasoned dried breadcrumbs

2 tablespoons chopped fresh parsley

4 ounces Parmesan cheese, grated

1. Preheat the oven to 350°F.

2. Remove the tails from the cleaned shrimp and cut the shrimp crosswise into thirds.

3. In a large saucepan, melt the butter over medium heat. Stir in the Cajun seasoning and minced onion. Add the shrimp and cook just until cooked through and no longer translucent in the center.

4. Remove the shrimp and set aside. Whisk the flour into the saucepan until well blended. Whisk in the milk, pouring it in a steady stream and whisking constantly. Let the mixture simmer for about 5 minutes, or until thickened.

5. Stir in the Cheddar and Monterey Jack cheeses and mix until they are melted and the sauce is smooth. Stir in the salt and pepper.

6. Add the cooked macaroni and stir to coat well. Return the shrimp to the pan and taste the sauce for seasoning. Add more salt, pepper, or Cajun seasoning if desired.

7. Spoon the mixture into a medium 2-quart casserole or a 9 x 13-inch baking dish and sprinkle the surface with the bread crumbs, parsley, and Parmesan.

8. Bake, uncovered, for 45 minutes, or until the top is browned and bubbling.

Makes 8 servings

This rich, creamy dish will fill up tummies fast. If leftovers aren't going to be devoured the next day, I suggest going ahead and freezing half and saving it for another night. Let the macaroni and cheese cool completely first, then place in a smaller freezer container.

BUCA DI BEPPO
Cheese Manicotti

BUCA DI BEPPO ISN'T KNOWN FOR SKIMPING ON THEIR PORTION SIZES. YOU CAN
REPLICATE THEIR FAMILY STYLE DISHES ECONOMICALLY AT HOME WITH THIS
HEARTY STUFFED PASTA AND ADJUST THE PORTION SIZES TO YOUR LIKING. US-
ING A PASTRY BAG WILL MAKE THE PROCESS OF FILLING THE MANICOTTI SHELLS
QUICK AND EASY.

Béchamel Sauce
2 tablespoons unsalted butter

¼ cup all-purpose flour

2 cups milk

1 teaspoon kosher salt

¼ teaspoon white pepper

¼ teaspoon ground nutmeg

Pasta Filling
1½ cups ricotta cheese

2 eggs, well beaten

4 ounces mozzarella cheese,
shredded

4 ounces provolone cheese,
shredded

2 ounces Parmesan cheese,
shredded

1 teaspoon kosher salt

¼ cup chopped fresh flat-leaf
parsley

Assembly
8 manicotti shells, cooked
according to package directions

1 to 2 cups marinara sauce,
store-bought or homemade

4 ounces mozzarella cheese,
shredded

1. **Make the béchamel sauce:** In a medium saucepan, melt the butter
   over low heat. Whisk in the flour and stir until smooth and just lightly
   colored.
2. Whisking constantly, pour the milk into the saucepan in a steady stream.
   Bring the heat up to medium until the liquid comes to a low boil, then
   reduce the heat again and simmer, stirring occasionally, until the mixture
   has thickened. Stir in the salt, pepper, and nutmeg. Keep the sauce warm.

3. **Make the pasta filling:** In a large bowl, whisk together the ricotta and eggs. Stir in the mozzarella, provolone, and Parmesan. Season with the salt and stir in the parsley.

4. **Assemble the manicotti:** Preheat the oven to 375°F.

5. Fill a large pastry bag with the pasta filling and pipe it into each of the cooked manicotti shells.

6. Use as much of the marinara sauce as needed to cover the bottom of a casserole or baking dish that is just large enough to hold the stuffed shells in a single layer. Place the manicotti in the baking dish, then spoon the béchamel sauce over the top and sides. Sprinkle with the mozzarella.

7. Bake, uncovered, for 25 to 30 minutes, or until the top is browned and bubbling.

8. Let the casserole sit for about 5 minutes before serving.

Makes 4 to 6 servings

Add some protein by adding cooked ground beef or crumbled Italian sausage to the filling!

BUCA DI BEPPO
Spaghetti and Meatballs

GROWN-UPS WHO FREQUENT BUCA DI BEPPO WILL RECOGNIZE THIS RECIPE AS A RESTAURANT CLASSIC. LITTLE ONES WILL THINK OF IT AS A FANCIER VERSION OF THEIR USUAL WEEKNIGHT MEAL.

Meatballs

2½ pounds ground meats (a mix of beef, veal, and pork is ideal)

4 ounces Pecorino Romano cheese, grated

¾ cup dried Italian bread crumbs

4 eggs, well beaten

2 teaspoons kosher salt

¼ cup minced garlic

Meatball Sauce

¼ cup extra virgin olive oil

6 large cloves garlic, sliced

1 cup coarsely chopped yellow onion

1 rib celery, chopped

1 carrot, peeled and chopped

¼ cup chopped flat-leaf parsley

2 (28-ounce) cans crushed plum tomatoes

1 tablespoon kosher salt

1 tablespoon pepper

Spaghetti

1 pound spaghetti, cooked according to package directions

4 ounces Parmesan

¼ cup shredded fresh basil

1. **Make the meatballs:** In a large bowl, combine the ground meats, Pecorino Romano, bread crumbs, eggs, salt, and garlic. Use your hands to thoroughly blend the ingredients. Shape into portions the size of a golf ball.

2. Set the meatballs on a large tray and refrigerate, covered, for at least 1 hour, or until you are ready to finish the dish.

3. **Make the meatball sauce:** In an 8-quart stockpot or 4-quart crockery, heat the olive oil. Add the sliced garlic, onion, celery, and carrot and cook until softened and just lightly browned. Stir in the parsley. Add the crushed tomatoes, salt, and pepper. Bring the sauce to a boil, then reduce the heat and let simmer for 20 minutes. Carefully add the meatballs.

4. Simmer the meatballs in the sauce for at least 1 hour, stirring occasionally and making sure the meatballs are turned over once or twice during cooking.

5. Serve the meatballs with the sauce over the cooked spaghetti. Sprinkle with the grated Parmesan and shredded basil.

Makes 12 servings

This is a large amount of food. One or two meatballs and a small portion of spaghetti might be more than enough for your littlest diner. You might want to portion out the meatballs and sauce in separate containers and freeze them for later use.

BURGER KING
French Toast Sticks

FOR BREAKFAST ON THE GO, BURGER KING'S FRENCH TOAST IS THE ULTIMATE PORTABLE MEAL. A SERVING OF TWO OR THREE GOLDEN PIECES JUST BEG TO BE DIPPED IN OOEY GOOEY MAPLE SYRUP OR SPREAD WITH A SMALL DOLLOP OF JAM. A SPRINKLING OF POWDERED SUGAR IS THE PERFECT FINISHING TOUCH.

2 thick slices white bread, crusts removed
½ cup egg whites
2 tablespoons sugar
1 teaspoon vanilla-flavored nondairy coffee creamer
½ teaspoon ground cinnamon
½ teaspoon vanilla extract
¼ teaspoon kosher salt
2 tablespoons unsalted butter
Maple syrup, for dipping

1. Toast the trimmed bread in a toaster or under the broiler. Cut each slice into four or five pieces.

2. In a shallow bowl, whisk together the egg whites, sugar, coffee creamer, cinnamon, vanilla, and salt.

3. In a large nonstick skillet, melt the butter over medium-high heat. Dip the toast pieces in the egg mixture, thoroughly coating all sides. Fry them in the hot butter, turning once, until golden on all sides.

4. Serve hot with maple syrup on the side for dipping, as they do at Burger King, or serve them on a plate with your favorite topping.

Makes 2 or 3 servings

A healthier option would be to go with a whole-grain bread studded with nuts and seeds.

BURGER KING
Chicken Fries

SIMILAR TO CHICKEN FINGERS, THESE CRUNCHY BITES ARE PERFECT COPYCATS OF THE ORIGINAL.

I egg
I tablespoon cold water
I pound chicken tenders, cut into strips similar to French fries
½ cup all-purpose flour

½ cup spice mix, such as Zatarain's Chicken Frying Mix
3 to 4 cups canola oil
Dipping sauces, such as barbecue, honey mustard, ranch dressing, or ketchup

1. In a bowl, beat together the egg and water.
2. Dip each piece of chicken into the egg wash and then into the flour.
3. Put the dry spice mix into a resealable plastic bag and shake a few of the floured chicken pieces in it until all are well coated, working in batches to season all the chicken.
4. Heat the oil in a large, heavy-bottomed saucepan or electric fryer.
5. Fry the chicken in batches until all are cooked through and they are golden brown on all sides. Drain on paper towels.
6. Serve with your favorite dipping sauce.

Makes 4 servings

You could use boneless, skinless chicken breasts. Just butterfly them open and cut into strips as described above.

CAFE RIO
Shredded Chicken Tacos

A SLOW COOKER IS AN ACTIVE FAMILY'S BEST FRIEND. LET IT DO THE WORK WHILE YOU PLAY (OR DO OTHER WORK). THEN LET THE TACO PARTY BEGIN!

2½ pounds boneless, skinless chicken breasts
¾ cup chicken broth
½ cup zesty Italian dressing, store-bought or homemade
1 tablespoon fresh lime juice
1 tablespoon chili powder
1 tablespoon dried minced onion
1 tablespoon granulated garlic

1 teaspoon ground cumin
1 teaspoon paprika
1 teaspoon kosher salt
½ teaspoon black pepper
¼ teaspoon cayenne pepper, or more to taste
1 dozen 6-inch corn or flour tortillas

Toppings

Shredded Monterey Jack cheese
Shredded Cheddar cheese
Fresh salsa or pico de gallo
Hot sauce, such as Tabasco

Guacamole
Chopped tomatoes
Chopped fresh cilantro
Shredded lettuce

1. Place the chicken breasts in the bottom of a slow cooker and cover them with the chicken broth.

2. In a bowl, whisk together the Italian dressing, lime juice, chili powder, dried onion, garlic, cumin, paprika, salt, black pepper, and cayenne. Pour the mixture over the chicken.

3. Cover the slow cooker, turn the setting to low, and cook for 6 to 8 hours. The chicken should pull apart easily with a fork. (If necessary, cook for another 30 minutes on high, or until it begins to fall apart.)

4. Either remove the chicken from the cooker to shred it, or shred it right in the cooker, with a fork.

5. To assemble the tacos, heat the tortillas in the oven or over a gas burner until warm. Spoon a portion of the chicken, drained of its cooking juices, in the center and add your favorite toppings. Fold into a taco and serve hot.

Makes 10 to 12 servings

CAFE RIO
Tres Leches Cake

"TRES LECHES" MEANS THREE MILKS. THIS TRADITIONAL MEXICAN CAKE IS SERVED
AT MANY CELEBRATIONS AND MAY BE THE MOISTEST CAKE YOU HAVE EVER EATEN.
IT TAKES ONLY LIGHTLY SWEETENED WHIPPED CREAM TO PUT A BEAUTIFUL FIN-
ISH ON YOUR FIESTA!

Cake
Shortening or cooking spray, for
   the pan
6 eggs, separated
2 cups sugar

2 cups all-purpose flour
2 teaspoons baking powder
½ cup milk
1 teaspoon vanilla extract

Cream Topping
1 (14-ounce) can evaporated milk
1 (14-ounce) can sweetened
   condensed milk

1 cup heavy (whipping) cream

Whipped Cream
1 pint heavy (whipping) cream
1 teaspoon vanilla extract

2 tablespoons powdered sugar,
   sifted

1. **Make the cake:** Preheat the oven to 350°F. Lightly coat a 9 x 13-inch
   baking pan with shortening or cooking spray and generously flour it.

2. In a bowl, with an electric mixer, beat the egg whites until soft peaks
   form. With the mixer running, gradually beat the sugar into the whites.
   Increase the speed and whip to stiff peaks. Add the yolks, one at a time,
   beating after each addition.

3. In a separate bowl, whisk together the flour and baking powder.

4. Add the dry ingredients to the whipped mixture a little at a time, beating
   in between additions so that the batter does not lose its volume. Beat in
   the milk and vanilla.

5. Pour the batter into the prepared pan and bake for 25 minutes, or until golden on top.

6. **Meanwhile, make the cream topping:** In a blender, combine the evaporated and condensed milks. With the motor running on high, pour in the heavy cream.

7. Remove the cake from the oven, and while it is still warm, poke a few holes in the cake and then pour the cream topping over the entire cake. Let the cake cool to room temperature, then cover and refrigerate until it is well chilled, at least 4 hours or overnight.

8. **Make the whipped cream:** Chill a clean metal bowl. Pour in the heavy (whipping) cream. Using an electric mixer, start on low speed, then increase it to high and whip the cream to soft peaks. With the mixer running, beat in the vanilla and powdered sugar. Continue beating until stiff peaks form.

9. Frost the chilled cake on the top only, or carefully remove it from the baking dish and frost the sides as well.

10. Keep refrigerated until ready to serve.

Makes 12 servings

You can make the whipped cream frosting a little sweeter by adding more powdered sugar. You can also bring some color to this dessert by adding a few drops of food coloring to the whipped cream as you're beating in the vanilla extract.

CALIFORNIA PIZZA KITCHEN
BBQ Chicken Pizza

THIS HAS BEEN A FAVORITE AT CALIFORNIA PIZZA KITCHEN SO LONG IT'S HARD TO REMEMBER THE TIME WHEN IT WASN'T ON THE MENU! A HOMEMADE PIZZA CRUST IS ALWAYS THE BEST, BUT A PURCHASED SHELL OR FROZEN/REFRIGERATED DOUGH IS PERFECT IN A PINCH. PREMADE PIZZA DOUGH ALSO COMES IN WHOLE WHEAT FOR A HEALTHIER OPTION.

Pizza Crust
1 teaspoon active dry yeast
1½ cups warm water
4 cups all-purpose flour
3 teaspoons kosher salt

½ cup olive oil
Vegetable oil, for the bowl
1 tablespoon cornmeal

BBQ Chicken
2 (8-ounce) boneless, skinless
chicken breasts
2 teaspoons kosher salt

½ cup barbecue sauce, store-
bought or homemade

Pizza Assembly
½ cup barbecue sauce
2 cups shredded mozzarella
cheese

1 small red onion, thinly sliced
(optional)
Fresh chopped cilantro (optional)

1. **Make the pizza crust:** Sprinkle the yeast over the warm water and set it aside until the yeast is activated, about 5 minutes.

2. In a stand mixer fitted with the dough hook, whisk together the flour and 1 teaspoon of salt. With the mixer running on low speed, drizzle in ⅓ cup of olive oil and mix just until the oil and flour are combined.

3. Slowly add the yeast mixture and beat until the dough becomes a sticky ball.

4. Lightly coat a clean bowl with vegetable oil and transfer the dough to the bowl. Cover the bowl with plastic wrap and set aside in a warm spot until the dough is doubled in size, at least 1 hour and possibly longer.

5. Punch down the risen dough and divide it into 2 pieces. Wrap one tightly in plastic wrap and refrigerate for future use.

6. Lightly flour a work surface and stretch the remaining dough into a 12- to 14-inch round crust, building up the edges to make a rim that will keep the toppings from melting off. Sprinkle 1 tablespoon of olive oil and the remaining kosher salt over the surface.

7. Drizzle a baking sheet with 1 tablespoon of olive oil and sprinkle it with the cornmeal. Slide the pizza crust on top. Let it sit while preparing the chicken.

8. **Make the BBQ chicken:** Preheat the oven to 350°F.

9. Season the chicken breasts with salt. Coat them on all sides with the barbecue sauce and lay them in a baking dish. Cover with foil and bake for 20 to 25 minutes, or until cooked through. When cool enough to handle, cut the chicken into cubes or thin strips. Leave the oven on and increase the oven temperature to 500°F.

10. **Assemble the pizza:** Spread the barbecue sauce evenly over the crust and sprinkle the mozzarella on top. Follow with the chicken and arrange the sliced red onion (if using) over the top. (Note that red onion has a very strong flavor kids might not like. While including it will more accurately mimic the taste of the original, defer to the littlest ones in the family!)

11. Bake the pizza for 15 to 20 minutes, or until the crust is golden and the cheese is bubbling and browned. Top with chopped cilantro, if desired.

12. Let the finished pizza sit for a minute then cut into wedges and serve hot.

Makes 10 to 12 servings

Keep in mind that this pizza dough can be made as many as 4 days ahead of time, if kept well bundled in plastic wrap and refrigerated. Cutting the finished pizza in small squares will increase the number of servings. Perfect for birthday parties and picnics!

CALIFORNIA PIZZA KITCHEN
Chicken Alfredo Pizza

INDULGE IN A POPULAR VERSION OF THE TRADITIONAL WHITE PIZZA. RICH WITH CREAM AND CHEESE, THIS PIZZA IS BEST SERVED IN SMALL BITES—GREAT FOR A DECADENT AFTER-SCHOOL SNACK OR DINNER WITH A SALAD.

Alfredo Sauce
2 tablespoons unsalted butter
1 teaspoon granulated garlic
1 teaspoon dried minced onion
1 tablespoon all-purpose flour
⅔ cup milk

⅔ cup heavy (whipping) cream
¼ cup grated Parmesan cheese
½ teaspoon kosher salt
¼ teaspoon white pepper

Pizza Dough and Topping
1 tablespoon all-purpose flour
16 ounces pizza dough, store-bought or homemade (from BBQ Chicken Pizza page 67)
1 tablespoon cornmeal
1½ cups shredded roasted or grilled chicken breast

1 cup shredded mozzarella cheese
6 thick slices smoked bacon, chopped and cooked to crisp
1 tablespoon extra virgin olive oil
2 green onions, thinly sliced (optional)

1. **Make the Alfredo sauce:** In a medium saucepan, melt the butter and stir in the granulated garlic and dried onion until blended. Whisk in the flour and let it cook until very lightly browned. Slowly whisk in the milk and then the cream, stirring constantly. Let the mixture come to a low boil and let it cook for about 20 minutes, stirring frequently.

2. When the sauce has thickened, remove it from the heat. Stir in the Parmesan, salt, and white pepper. Keep the sauce warm while finishing the pizza.

3. **Make the pizza:** Preheat the oven to 425°F. If you have a pizza stone, place it on the rack in the center of the oven to heat up for at least 30 minutes.

4. Sprinkle the flour on a work surface, then shape the pizza dough into a 12- to 14-inch round crust, building up the edges to make a rim that will keep the toppings from melting off.

5. Sprinkle a baking sheet with the cornmeal. Carefully transfer the crust to the baking sheet and spread it evenly with half the cream sauce, leaving about 1 inch bare at the edge.

6. Arrange the cooked chicken over the top, then cover evenly with the remaining cream sauce. Sprinkle the top evenly with the mozzarella and then sprinkle with the cooked bacon.

7. Brush the outer edges of the crust with the olive oil. Bake for 15 to 20 minutes, or until the crust is evenly golden. Sprinkle with the green onions (if using) before serving. (Note that green onion has a very strong flavor kids might not like. While including it will more accurately mimic the taste of the original, defer to the littlest ones in the family!)

8. Let the pizza sit for just a minute before slicing into wedges or squares.

Makes 10 to 12 servings

There's no law that says pizza has to be round. Shape the dough into a 12-inch square and use a pizza wheel or sharp knife to slice it any way you choose. Using whole wheat flour will make the crust a little denser and chewier and will contribute a higher nutritive value over the all-purpose flour.

CALIFORNIA PIZZA KITCHEN
Curly Mac 'n' Cheese

TO ADD A BIT MORE NUTRITION TO THEIR CHEESY PASTA, CALIFORNIA PIZZA KITCHEN TOSSES THIS DISH WITH EDAMAME (STEAMED SOYBEANS) AND WILL ALSO MAKE IT WITH MULTIGRAIN PASTA ON REQUEST. YOU CAN DO THE SAME AT HOME TO ADD CRUNCH AND TEXTURE TO A VERY RICH MEAL.

1½ cups heavy (whipping) cream
2 tablespoons unsalted butter
½ pound Velveeta cheese, cut
   into small cubes

1 pound fusilli pasta, cooked
   according to package directions

1. In a large saucepan, heat the heavy cream over medium heat and stir in the butter.
2. Reduce the heat and stir in the cubed Velveeta, a few pieces at a time.
3. When all the cheese has melted, stir in the cooked pasta and coat it well with the cheese sauce. Serve hot.

Makes 6 to 8 servings

Add some green to this dish with chopped fresh parsley sprinkled over the top just before serving. Or to make grown-ups happy, spoon fresh basil and tomato sauce over the top and serve as a casserole, but don't mention you got the recipe from the kids' menu!

CHARLEY'S GRILLED SUBS

Philly Cheesesteak

EVERYONE LOVES A PHILLY CHEESESTEAK SANDWICH, AND CHARLEY'S MAKES ONE
OF THE BEST. YOU CAN DUPLICATE THEIR FAMOUSLY FILLING SANDWICH AT HOME
USING FRESH, QUALITY INGREDIENTS.

1 pound lean beef, such as top
round, thinly sliced
Kosher salt and pepper
2 tablespoons olive oil

1 yellow onion, cut into ¼-inch
slices
½ cup shredded provolone
cheese
2 hoagie rolls, split and toasted

1. Season the beef with salt and pepper.

2. In a cast-iron or heavy-bottomed skillet, heat the oil over medium heat.
   Add the onion and cook until lightly golden. Remove from the skillet
   and set aside. Add the seasoned meat and cook quickly, just until no
   longer pink.

3. Sprinkle the provolone over the meat while it is still in the pan, and toss
   gently until the cheese is melted.

4. Pile the cheese and meat onto the bottoms of each roll and top with the
   cooked onion. Close with the top bun and serve hot.

Makes 2 servings

*These are large sandwiches. For smaller kids, you may want to
split the sandwiches in half, or make 4 sandwiches with the
same amount of ingredients but with smaller buns.*

CHEDDAR'S
Baked Spasagna

THIS IS NOT A TYPO! CHEDDAR'S REALLY SERVES THIS COMBINATION OF SPAGHETTI AND LASAGNA TO HUNGRY CUSTOMERS WHO WANT THE CREAMINESS OF CHEESY LASAGNA WITH THE TEXTURE OF SPAGHETTI PASTA. THIS IS A GREAT DISH TO SPLIT AND FREEZE FOR LATER.

Cooking spray

2 pounds mozzarella cheese, grated

1 cup ricotta cheese

1 cup sour cream

1 cup half-and-half

½ cup grated Parmesan cheese

1 teaspoon granulated garlic

1 teaspoon dried basil

1 teaspoon dried oregano

1 teaspoon kosher salt

½ teaspoon pepper

1½ pounds spaghetti, cooked according to package directions

3½ cups spaghetti sauce, store-bought or homemade

1 pound sweet Italian sausage, crumbled and browned

1. Preheat the oven to 350°F. Lightly coat a 9 x 13-inch baking dish with cooking spray.

2. In a large bowl, combine the mozzarella, ricotta, sour cream, half-and-half, ¼ cup of the Parmesan, the garlic, basil, oregano, salt, and pepper and stir until well blended. Add the cooked spaghetti and toss until it is well coated.

3. Pour the mixture into the baking dish and sprinkle with the remaining ¼ cup Parmesan. Cover the dish with foil and bake for 30 minutes.

4. Meanwhile, heat the spaghetti sauce and the cooked sausage in a saucepan over medium heat. Let it simmer over low heat for about 20 minutes.

5. When the spasagna is cooked, remove the foil and let it sit for about 15 minutes, then cut it into squares and spoon the warm meat sauce over the top.

Makes 10 to 12 servings

This can be quite a crowd-pleaser! Consider cutting smaller portions and serving with a salad or two and a simple dessert for a buffet or party.

THE CHEESECAKE FACTORY
Whipped Potatoes

BUTTERY WHIPPED POTATOES GO WITH ALMOST EVERYTHING AND ARE RARELY LEFT OVER. THE CHEESECAKE FACTORY MAKES CREAMY SKIN-ON MASHED RED POTATOES AND REAL BUTTER.

6 medium red potatoes, quartered

4 tablespoons (½ stick) unsalted butter, cut into chunks

1 teaspoon kosher salt, or more to taste

½ teaspoon white pepper

1 cup heavy (whipping) cream, heated to warm

1. Put the potatoes in a large pot with cold water to cover. Bring to a boil and cook until the potatoes are cooked through but still firm, about 20 minutes.
2. Drain the potatoes and return them to the pot. Add the butter, salt, and pepper.
3. Use a hand-mixer or large whisk to whip the potatoes. Add enough of the heavy cream to make the potatoes smooth.
4. Taste and adjust the salt and pepper if necessary and keep warm.

Makes 4 to 6 servings

Using a stand mixer with the whisk attachment is the quickest way to whip potatoes. Put the boiled potatoes into the bowl of the mixer and add the butter and seasonings. Start the mixer on a low speed and add the cream gradually until you reach the desired consistency.

THE CHEESECAKE FACTORY

Parmesan Polenta Fries

SERVE THESE CHEESY TREATS INSTEAD OF FRENCH FRIES! POLENTA, OR FINELY GROUND CORNMEAL, WILL STAY FRESH IN THE CUPBOARD FOR MONTHS, SO CONSIDER IT A STAPLE.

2 cups milk

4 cups chicken broth

2 tablespoons unsalted butter

3¼ cups quick-cooking polenta

½ cup grated Parmesan cheese

¼ cup chopped fresh parsley

1 teaspoon kosher salt

½ teaspoon pepper

3 to 4 cups canola or vegetable shortening, for deep-frying

1. In a large saucepan, combine the milk, broth, and butter. Bring to a rolling boil and slowly stir in the polenta in a steady stream. Reduce the heat and stir until the polenta pulls away from the sides of the pan. Stir in the Parmesan, parsley, salt, and pepper.

2. Lightly coat a baking sheet with a little oil and spread the polenta in an even layer over the surface of the pan. Refrigerate for at least 1 hour, or until cold throughout.

3. In a heavy-bottomed saucepan or electric fryer, heat the oil to 350°F (use a deep-fry thermometer).

4. Cut the chilled polenta into "fries," ¾-inch wide by about 3 inches long. Working in batches, fry in the hot oil until crispy. Drain on a wire rack or on paper towels. Serve hot.

Makes 8 servings

These fried sticks make excellent dippers for parties and play dates. Line a basket with a napkin and cover them to keep warm. Serve with warm marinara sauce or a creamy cheese dip.

THE CHEESECAKE FACTORY
Pasta with Mushroom Bolognese

THIS CLASSIC, RICH SAUCE CAN BE MADE MEATLESS WITHOUT SACRIFICING FLAVOR. THE CHEESECAKE FACTORY USES SPAGHETTINI FOR THIS DISH, BUT YOU CAN USE THE PASTA OF YOUR CHOICE.

2 tablespoons olive oil

¼ cup finely chopped peeled carrot

¼ cup finely chopped onion

3 large cloves garlic, minced

¾ cup mushrooms, stemmed and sliced

1 teaspoon kosher salt

¼ teaspoon pepper

2 teaspoons minced fresh thyme

¼ cup sherry or Marsala

1¼ cups marinara sauce, store-bought or homemade

2 tablespoons unsalted butter

8 ounces spaghettini, cooked according to package directions

¼ cup grated Parmesan cheese

2 tablespoons chopped fresh parsley

1. In a large skillet, heat the oil over medium heat. Add the carrot, onion, and garlic. Sauté the vegetables for 2 or 3 minutes, or until softened.

2. Stir in the sliced mushrooms and season the mixture with salt and pepper. Let the vegetables simmer, stirring frequently until the mushrooms give up their liquid. Reduce the heat to medium-low. Add the thyme and sherry. Let the mixture cook down until almost dry, stirring frequently.

3. Stir in the marinara sauce and scrape up any browned bits left on the bottom of the pan. Simmer for about 5 minutes, or until the sauce is heated through.

4. Stir in the butter, a tablespoon at a time, until it is melted and blended in. Add the cooked pasta and let it heat through. Sprinkle with half the Parmesan and toss.

5. Just before serving, sprinkle with the parsley and remaining Parmesan.

* * * * * * * * * *

Makes 4 servings

* * * * * * * * * *

Porcini mushrooms are among the most aromatic in the world. Although only available fresh during a short season, they are often dried for later rehydration. To give this sauce a deep mushroom flavor, soak an ounce of dried porcini mushrooms in 2 cups warm water for 20 minutes, then chop them and add them to the sauce when you add the marinara. Strain the soaking water and add it as well, as it will have picked up the intense flavor of the mushrooms.

CHEVYS FRESH MEX
Sweet Corn Tomalito

VERY SIMILAR TO SWEET CORN TAMALES, THIS TEMPTING DISH FROM CHEVYS CAN
SERVE AS AN ENTRÉE OR SIDE DISH. LOOK FOR MASA HARINA IN THE LATIN FOODS
AISLE OF LARGER MARKETS.

5 tablespoons margarine,
 softened
¼ cup masa harina
½ cup regular cornmeal
¼ cup sugar

2 cups corn kernels, fresh or
 thawed frozen
½ cup water or chicken broth
½ teaspoon baking powder
½ teaspoon kosher salt
½ cup milk

1. Assemble a steamer that will fit an 8-inch square baking dish: Place a
   wire rack in the bottom of a large saucepan or soup pot. Fill with water
   just up to the height of the rack. If your rack does not sit very high off
   the bottom of the pot, use a few sturdy glass jars to suspend the rack.
   You should have at least 2 inches of water in the pot before it touches the
   rim of the rack.

2. Bring the water to a low simmer while you are preparing the tomalito.

3. In a medium bowl, with an electric mixer, beat together the margarine,
   masa, cornmeal, and sugar until light and fluffy.

4. In a blender, puree 1 cup of the corn kernels with the water or broth until smooth. Stir the corn puree into the masa mixture and stir well. Add
   the remaining corn kernels along with the baking powder, salt, and milk.
   Stir until mixed.

5. Pour the corn mixture into the 8-inch square baking dish and wrap
   tightly with plastic. Place it on the rack in the "steamer."

6. Bring the water to a boil and cover the pot. Steam the tomalito for 50 to 60 minutes, checking occasionally to see if the pot needs more water. A toothpick inserted into the center of the tomalito should come out clean when it is ready.

7. Remove the plastic and let the tomalito sit for at least 5 minutes before cutting and serving.

Makes 6 servings

Larger portions can be served with fresh pico de gallo, green chile salsa, or chili con carne for a filling entrée. Smaller pieces can be cut for an appetizer or child-size bites.

CHICK-FIL-A
Chocolate Chunk Cookies

THESE ARE LIKE THE OLD-FASHIONED COOKIES MADE IN AMERICAN HOUSEHOLDS BEFORE CONVENIENCE FOODS TOOK OVER. YOU'LL NEED TO INVEST IN SEVERAL INGREDIENTS, BUT THE RESULTS WILL BE WORTH IT!

½ cup solid vegetable shortening
8 tablespoons (1 stick) unsalted butter, still cool but not right out of the fridge
½ cup granulated sugar
½ cup packed dark brown sugar
2 eggs
½ cup light corn syrup
½ teaspoon maple syrup
¼ cup milk
3 cups all-purpose flour

1 teaspoon kosher salt
1 teaspoon baking powder
½ teaspoon baking soda
½ teaspoon ground cinnamon
¼ teaspoon ground ginger
1½ cups rolled oats
6 ounces bittersweet chocolate chunks or chips
6 ounces milk chocolate chunks or chips

1. In a bowl, with an electric mixer, beat together the shortening and butter until smooth. Add the granulated and brown sugars, then beat until light and fluffy. Beat in the eggs one at a time, until well incorporated. Mix in the corn syrup, maple syrup, and milk.

2. In a separate bowl, whisk together the flour, salt, baking powder, baking soda, cinnamon, and ginger. Gradually stir the flour mixture into the batter.

3. With a wooden spoon, stir in the rolled oats, then mix in the two types of chocolate chunks or chips. If the dough seems too thick to stir, you can thin it out with a little extra milk; the dough should remain loose enough to easily scoop.

4. Refrigerate the dough for at least 30 minutes so it can firm up.

5. Preheat the oven to 350°F. Line a baking sheet with parchment paper.

6. Use an ice cream scoop or a tablespoon to drop mounds of dough on the prepared baking sheet, placing them at least 2 inches apart. You may need another baking sheet if one is not large enough.

7. Bake the cookies for 10 to 12 minutes. Let them cool briefly on the pan, then transfer to a wire rack to cool completely. Store in an airtight container.

Makes about 3 dozen cookies

For a nice variation, add ½ cup chopped pecans or walnuts when you stir in the chocolate chips.

CHICK-FIL-A
Fruit Cup

SOMETIMES SOMETHING AS SIMPLE AS A FRUIT CUP CAN BE JUST THE THING TO FILL A HUNGRY TUMMY. USE OTHER FRUITS THAT ARE IN SEASON IF THOSE LISTED BELOW AREN'T AVAILABLE.

1 red apple, such as Red Delicious, cored and cubed

1 green apple, such as Granny Smith, cored and cubed

Juice of 1 lemon

1 orange, peeled, segmented, and chopped

1 cup strawberries, hulled and quartered

1 cup blueberries, fresh or thawed frozen

2 tablespoons sugar

1. In a large bowl, toss the cubed apples with the lemon juice to keep them from discoloring. Add the remaining fruits and toss.
2. Sprinkle with the sugar and divide into serving portions. Cover and refrigerate any leftovers.

Makes 4 to 6 servings

Substitute the orange with canned mandarin orange segments or seedless tangerines. Seedless red or green grapes are fine in place of the strawberries. Blackberries are also a good alternative.

CHICK-FIL-A
Nuggets

GOT PICKY EATERS AT HOME? CONVINCE THE KIDS THAT YOU PICKED UP THEIR FAVORITE MENU ITEM FROM CHICK-FIL-A, WHEN YOU REALLY SAVED A BUNDLE AND MADE THEM YOURSELF. LOOK FOR GOOD PRICES ON CHICKEN TENDERS. REFRIGERATE WHAT YOU NEED FOR ONE MEAL AND FREEZE THE REST FOR ANOTHER TIME.

1 egg
1 cup milk
2 pounds chicken tenders, cut into bite-size pieces
1 cup all-purpose flour, plus more as needed
2 tablespoons powdered sugar
1 teaspoon granulated garlic

1 teaspoon kosher salt
½ teaspoon pepper
½ teaspoon paprika
2 to 3 cups vegetable oil, for deep-frying
Chick-fil-A Sauce (recipe follows)

1. In a shallow bowl, beat the egg. Whisk in the milk. Add the chicken pieces to the mixture and turn them to thoroughly coat. Cover the bowl and refrigerate for at least 4 hours.

2. In a large resealable plastic bag, combine the flour, powdered sugar, garlic, salt, pepper, and paprika.

3. Drain the chicken from the milk marinade and discard the marinade.

4. Fill a heavy-bottomed saucepan or electric fryer halfway with the vegetable oil and heat to between 350° and 375°F (use a deep-fry thermometer).

5. Toss the chicken pieces in the flour mixture, coating completely. Working in batches, fry the chicken until cooked through and golden on all sides. Drain the nuggets on paper towels and serve hot.

6. Serve Chick-fil-A sauce for dipping.

Makes 4 to 6 servings

Chick-fil-A Sauce

1 cup mayonnaise

2 teaspoons sugar

¼ cup barbecue sauce, store-bought or homemade

¼ cup real maple syrup

¼ cup apple cider vinegar

¼ teaspoon liquid smoke flavoring

½ teaspoon onion powder

½ teaspoon granulated garlic

2 tablespoons yellow mustard

Whisk all ingredients together in a small bowl, and refrigerate in a tightly sealed glass jar until needed.

Makes about 1¾ cups

CHILI'S
Cinnamon Apples

CHILI'S OFFERS THIS ITEM AS A SIDE DISH, BUT IT MAKES A GREAT LIGHT DESSERT FOR KIDS. SAVE THE LEFTOVERS FOR TOPPING BREAKFAST CEREAL OR PANCAKES.

8 to 9 Granny Smith apples
1 tablespoon fresh lemon juice
½ cup sugar
2 tablespoons cornstarch
2 tablespoons ground cinnamon
½ teaspoon ground allspice
½ teaspoon ground nutmeg
¼ teaspoon kosher salt
2 tablespoons unsalted butter, diced

1. Peel, core, and slice the apples and toss them with the lemon juice in a large bowl.

2. In a small bowl, whisk together the sugar, cornstarch, cinnamon, allspice, nutmeg, and salt. Sprinkle the spices over the apples and toss to coat them well.

3. Place the apples in a microwave-safe dish and dot with the butter. Cover the dish and microwave on high for 10 to 15 minutes, stopping and stirring them twice. The apples should be cooked through but not mushy.

Makes 8 to 10 servings

If desired, spoon the apples into individual ramekins before topping with butter. You may need to microwave them in batches, just remember to stir each one a couple of times during cooking. Jazz it up with a dollop of sweetened whipped cream or frozen topping and a sprinkling of nuts.

CHILI'S
Grilled Chicken Platter

THIS PLATTER MAKES A WONDERFUL PRESENTATION AT THE DINNER TABLE. THE PUEBLO RICE IS BRIMMING WITH FRESH VEGETABLES, AND THE CHICKEN IS HOT AND JUICY RIGHT OFF THE GRILL. SAVE SOME TIME BY GETTING THE VEGETABLES PREPPED AND READY TO GO—YOU CAN EVEN MAKE THE RICE AHEAD OF TIME AND GENTLY REHEAT IT BEFORE SERVING.

Pueblo Rice

2 tablespoons olive oil

2 tablespoons unsalted butter

⅔ cup diced yellow onion

¾ cup chopped celery

½ cup peeled, chopped carrot

1 teaspoon seasoned salt, such as Lawry's

½ cup pineapple juice

2¼ cups chicken broth

1½ cups long-grain white rice

½ cup diced mixed bell peppers—red, green, and yellow

Chicken and Vegetables

Vegetable oil

4 (6-ounce) boneless, skinless chicken breasts

Kosher salt and pepper

1 cup chopped zucchini

1 cup chopped yellow squash

½ cup chopped yellow onion

½ cup chopped red bell pepper

½ cup chopped green bell pepper

2 ears corn, husked and split in half crosswise

¼ cup grated Parmesan cheese

1. **Make the pueblo rice:** In a large saucepan, heat the oil and butter over medium heat. Add the onion, celery, and carrot and sauté until cooked through but not browned.

2. Sprinkle with the seasoned salt, then stir in the pineapple juice and chicken broth. Bring to a boil, then add the rice and mixed bell peppers. When the liquid returns to a boil, cover the pot and reduce the heat to very low. Cook the rice until tender, about 20 minutes, then remove from the heat and set aside.

3. **Cook the chicken and vegetables:** Preheat the grill to high. Lightly coat the grates with vegetable oil.

4. Season the chicken breasts with salt and pepper and grill them about 4 minutes per side, until cooked through, turning once.

5. Meanwhile, place the zucchini, yellow squash, onion, and bell peppers in a microwave-safe dish. Add 2 or 3 tablespoons of water and cover the dish. Microwave on high for about 6 minutes, or until the vegetables are cooked through but still nicely firm.

6. Grill the corn, turning often, until cooked through.

7. When the chicken is ready, fluff the rice with a fork and arrange it on the bottom of a large serving platter. Mound the steamed vegetables around the outside of the rice and sprinkle them with Parmesan.

8. Arrange the grilled corn on one side of the platter and the chicken breasts on the other. Serve hot.

Makes 4 servings

Grill the vegetables with a little olive oil, salt, and pepper if you prefer. Grill the squash whole and the onions in thick rings. Cut the tops and bottoms off the bell peppers and cut them in large slabs, removing the seeds and strips of veins from inside each pepper. When they are cool enough to handle, cut the cooked vegetables into bite-size pieces.

CHIPOTLE MEXICAN GRILL
Taco Kid's Meal

A FAMILY THAT BUILDS TACOS TOGETHER STAYS TOGETHER. AND STAYS HEALTHY!

3 ounces boneless, skinless
  chicken breast
Kosher salt and pepper
4 tablespoons lime juice
2 tablespoons chopped fresh
  cilantro
Oil
½ cup cooked rice

1 or 2 taco shells, store-bought
  or homemade
¼ cup shredded Monterey Jack
  cheese
Tortilla chips
Mild salsa
Guacamole

1. Season the chicken with salt and pepper. Place in a bowl and toss with 2 tablespoons of the lime juice and 1 tablespoon of the cilantro. Refrigerate it for at least 1 hour.

2. Preheat the broiler or grill to high heat and lightly oil the grates. Broil or grill the chicken until cooked through and no longer pink in the center. When cool, cut the chicken into a small dice.

3. Mix the cooked rice with the remaining 2 tablespoons lime juice and 1 tablespoon cilantro.

4. Serve each taco ingredient in a separate bowl for easy taco building.

Makes 1 serving

In place of the hard taco shells, you can gently warm corn tortillas over a stove burner or on the grill. Fold them in half and cover with a clean cloth to keep warm.

CINNABON
Caramel Pecanbon

CINNABON PRIDES ITSELF ON THE EXCELLENT INGREDIENTS THEY PROCURE FOR
THEIR SIGNATURE BAKED GOODS. A LUSCIOUS FACSIMILE CAN BE MADE USING
PREPARED BISCUIT DOUGH AND FRESHLY MADE PECAN TOPPING.

½ cup packed golden brown
   sugar
3 tablespoons unsalted butter
2 tablespoons honey
¾ cup chopped toasted pecans

1 (16-ounce) can refrigerated
   large buttermilk biscuits (8
   biscuits)
¼ cup granulated sugar
1½ teaspoons ground cinnamon

Glaze
1 tablespoon milk

⅓ cup powdered sugar

1. Preheat the oven to 400°F.
2. In a small saucepan, combine the brown sugar, 2 tablespoons of the butter, and honey and cook over low heat, stirring until the sugar is dissolved and the ingredients are well blended.
3. Pour the mixture over the bottom of a 9-inch cake pan and sprinkle the chopped pecans evenly.
4. In a small bowl, melt the remaining 1 tablespoon butter in the microwave for about 10 seconds. Brush each biscuit with the melted butter. Arrange the biscuits over the pecan mixture with the sides touching. Whisk together the granulated sugar and cinnamon and sprinkle it over the buttered biscuits.
5. Bake for 20 minutes, or until the tops of the biscuits are browned.
6. Set a wire rack over a sheet of wax paper and invert the cooked buns onto the rack.

7. **Make the glaze:** In a small bowl, stir the milk into the powdered sugar. Drizzle the glaze over the top of each bun and serve warm.

Makes 8 servings

Use this same method for making other buns with a variety of ingredients! Try walnuts instead of pecans and maple syrup instead of honey. If you have family members with nut allergies, make the same recipe but use raisins or chopped dried apples instead. Not that anyone making these sticky treasures is counting calories, but you can shave off a few by using reduced-fat biscuits and low-fat milk for the glaze.

CLAIM JUMPER
Baby Back Pork Ribs

CLAIM JUMPER MAY NOT USE THESE EXACT INGREDIENTS IN THEIR DELECTABLE BABY BACK RIBS, BUT I PROMISE THE FLAVOR IS NEARLY THE SAME.

1 (12-ounce) can regular Coca-Cola
1 (32-ounce) bottle Wishbone Italian dressing

1 tablespoon liquid smoke flavoring, such as Liquid Smoke
3 to 4 pounds baby back ribs, trimmed
Oil

1. In a bowl, whisk together the Coke, Italian dressing, and smoke flavoring.
2. Arrange the ribs in a pan large enough to fit them in a single layer and pour the mixture over them. Turn the ribs a couple of times to make sure all sides are marinated. Cover the pan and refrigerate at least 24 hours.
3. Preheat a grill to medium. Lightly oil the grates.
4. Remove the ribs from the marinade and reserve it as a basting sauce.
5. Grill the ribs over medium heat for about 90 minutes until tender, brushing often with the marinade.

Makes 4 to 6 servings

You can also use the Claim Jumper barbecue sauce, available at major retailers as well as at online stores, to baste the ribs.

COLD STONE CREAMERY
Sweet Cream Ice Cream

YOU'LL NEED AN ICE CREAM MAKER FOR THIS RECIPE, BUT THE PURCHASE WILL BE WELL WORTH THE EXPENSE. AFTER THE RAPID DISAPPEARANCE OF YOUR FIRST BATCH, YOU WILL BE GLAD TO HAVE IT ON HAND!

½ cup sugar, superfine if available
2 tablespoons cornstarch
2 cups heavy (whipping) cream

1 cup milk
¼ cup light corn syrup

Suggested flavorings

Chocolate chips
Chopped nuts
Candy sprinkles
Crushed cookies
Dried fruit

Chopped candy bars
Cereals or granola
Gummies
Cut-up peanut butter cups

1. In a small bowl, whisk together the sugar and cornstarch. In a medium saucepan, combine the heavy cream, milk, and corn syrup.

2. Add the dry ingredients to the cream mixture and bring it to a gentle boil, whisking frequently. Once it comes to a boil, stir constantly for about 30 seconds, then remove it from the heat.

3. Set up a fine-mesh sieve over a large bowl and strain the cream mixture into the bowl. Lay a sheet of plastic wrap over the surface of the cream mixture and refrigerate it until fully chilled. Transfer the covered bowl to the freezer and continue chilling for about 1 hour.

4. Pour the cold ice cream mixture into an ice cream maker and process according to the manufacturer's directions. Add any of the suggested flavorings during the last 5 minutes of processing in the ice cream maker.

5. Store the finished ice cream in an airtight container and freeze until firm.

Makes 4 to 6 servings

COPELAND'S
Jambalaya Pasta

TRADITIONAL JAMBALAYA IS USUALLY SERVED WITH RICE, BUT COPELAND'S STEPS UP THE WOW FACTOR BY SERVING IT OVER A GENEROUS PORTION OF PENNE. TINY TUMMIES MAY NOT BE USED TO SUCH RICHNESS, SO IT MAY BE BEST TO SERVE SMALL AMOUNTS.

1 tablespoon unsalted butter
½ cup cubed andouille sausage
½ cup cubed smoked pork sausage
1 (6-ounce) boneless, skinless chicken breast, cubed
¼ pound medium shrimp, peeled and deveined
½ cup sliced bell pepper (green, red, yellow, or a mix of all three)
½ cup thinly sliced white mushrooms
2 green onions (white parts only), sliced
1 teaspoon Creole seasoning, store-bought or homemade
¼ cup beef gravy
¼ cup tomato sauce
8 ounces penne pasta, cooked according to package directions

1. In a large skillet, melt the butter over medium heat. Add both sausages and cook until heated through. Add the chicken and cook thoroughly, then add the shrimp and cook just until they lose their translucence.

2. Stir in the bell peppers, mushrooms, green onions, and Creole seasoning. Simmer the mixture for a few minutes.

3. Stir in the gravy and tomato sauce and bring to a boil.

4. Add the cooked pasta, toss to mix all the ingredients, and serve hot.

Makes 4 to 6 servings

Copeland's likes penne for this dish because it is easier to deal with than long strands of spaghetti. You can also use fusilli, rotelli, or medium shells to capture the sauce of this savory stew.

COPELAND'S
Macaroni and Cheese

COPELAND'S STARTED IN NEW ORLEANS AND NOW HAS LOCATIONS IN TEXAS AND
OTHER PARTS OF THE SOUTH. THEY FEATURE CREOLE FAVORITES AND AUTHENTIC
NEW ORLEANS FLAVORS. THEIR KIDS' MENU FEATURES MAC AND CHEESE WITH A
TWIST—BOW-TIE PASTA.

4 tablespoons (½ stick) unsalted butter
5 tablespoons all-purpose flour
1 quart milk
1 pound sharp Cheddar cheese, shredded
½ teaspoon Tabasco sauce (optional)
1 teaspoon kosher salt
1 teaspoon dry mustard
½ teaspoon sweet paprika
½ teaspoon pepper
1 pound bow-tie pasta, cooked according to package directions
Cooking spray or butter, for the baking dish
2 tablespoons chopped fresh parsley

1. In a large saucepan, melt the butter over medium heat. Whisk in the flour and stir until smooth and only lightly colored. Gradually pour in the milk, whisking constantly, and bring to a boil. Reduce the heat, then simmer, stirring occasionally until thickened.

2. Remove the pan from the heat and stir in the Cheddar, Tabasco sauce (if using), salt, mustard, paprika, and pepper. Stir until the cheese is melted and the sauce is thick and creamy.

3. Stir the cooked bow-tie pasta into the cheese sauce and coat it thoroughly.

4. Preheat the broiler. Lightly coat a shallow 3-quart baking dish with cooking spray or butter.

5. Pour the mac and cheese into the prepared dish and place it under the hot broiler until bubbling and crusty. Sprinkle with parsley just before serving.

Makes 6 to 8 servings

*Even though Copeland's uses bow-tie pasta for this kids' dish,
you can use regular elbow macaroni if that is what you have on
hand.*

CRACKER BARREL
Peach Cobbler with Almond Crumble Topping

CRACKER BARREL GETS RAVE REVIEWS FOR THEIR PEACH COBBLER. SOME LOCATIONS ARE OFFERING COBBLERS MADE WITH BLACKBERRIES, AS WELL AS OTHER SEASONAL FRUITS. THEY USE THEIR OWN PANCAKE MIX TO MAKE THE COBBLER, AND YOU CAN TOO IF THERE IS A LOCATION NEAR YOU. IF NOT, TRY THIS RECIPE USING A STANDARD BAKING MIX.

Cooking spray or butter, for the baking dish
1¼ cups baking mix, such as Bisquick
1 cup milk

8 tablespoons (1 stick) unsalted butter, melted
½ teaspoon ground cinnamon
¼ teaspoon ground nutmeg

Filling
¼ cup granulated sugar

2 (15-ounce) cans sliced peaches in syrup, drained

Crumble Topping
¼ cup sliced almonds
½ cup packed golden brown sugar

½ teaspoon ground cinnamon
1 tablespoon unsalted butter, melted

1. Preheat the oven to 375°F. Lightly coat an 8-inch square baking dish with cooking spray or butter.

2. In a large bowl, combine the baking mix, milk, melted butter, cinnamon, and nutmeg and stir until well combined.

3. Pour the batter into the prepared dish and smooth it evenly from side to side.

4. **Make the filling:** In a bowl, toss the granulated sugar and peaches together. When they are well coated, arrange them over the top of the batter and bake for 45 minutes.

5. **Meanwhile, make the crumble topping:** In a bowl, toss the almonds with the brown sugar, cinnamon, and melted butter.

6. Sprinkle the topping over the peaches and bake for another 10 minutes. Let the cobbler sit a few minutes before serving.

Makes 8 or 9 servings

Enjoy this moist cobbler with a scoop of vanilla bean ice cream or with a dollop of freshly whipped and lightly sweetened cream.

DAIRY QUEEN
Peanut Buster Parfait

THE KIDS ARE GOING TO LOVE THIS CONFECTION OF HOT FUDGE, SOFT ICE CREAM, AND PEANUTS. THEY'LL BE GRABBING THEM AS SOON AS YOU CAN MAKE THEM!

1 cup hot fudge topping, warmed
1 pint vanilla ice cream, softened

¼ cup unsalted roasted Spanish peanuts

1. Using two 1½-cup glasses or sturdy plastic cups, pour 1 inch hot fudge into the bottom of each glass.
2. Fill the glass with the softened ice cream to about halfway.
3. Pour in another 1 inch of hot fudge, then fill to a little below the brim with more ice cream.
4. Finish off the top of the parfait with more hot fudge and a sprinkling of the peanuts.
5. Serve immediately.

Makes 2 servings

Soft-serve ice cream can only be made with a special machine that injects air into the mixture before freezing. Lightly softened regular ice cream will do for a simple sundae like this one. Any leftover ice cream can be hardened in the freezer. Extra hot fudge should be cooled first and refrigerated in a sealed container.

DAVE & BUSTER'S
Baked Chicken and Shrimp Alfredo

DAVE & BUSTER'S SERVES THIS BAKED DELIGHT WITH CAVATAPPI PASTA. ELBOW MACARONI OR FUSILLI PASTA MAY BE EASIER TO FIND IN THE GROCERY AISLE. ALTHOUGH NOT STRICTLY ON THE KIDS' MENU AT DAVE & BUSTER'S, THIS RECIPE IS PERFECT FOR SERVING UP IN SMALLER PORTIONS. LEFTOVERS WILL LAST UP TO 5 DAYS IF TIGHTLY WRAPPED AND REFRIGERATED.

Three-Cheese Alfredo Sauce
- 1 tablespoon unsalted butter
- 2 cloves garlic, minced
- 4 ounces cream cheese, softened
- 1 cup milk
- ½ cup shredded mozzarella cheese
- ¼ cup grated Parmesan cheese
- 1 teaspoon kosher salt
- ½ teaspoon pepper

Garlic Bread Crumb Crust
- 2 tablespoons unsalted butter, melted
- 2 tablespoons olive oil
- 2 teaspoons granulated garlic
- 2 cups dried bread crumbs, such as panko
- ¼ cup grated Parmesan cheese

Assembly and Baking
- 2 tablespoons olive oil
- 1½ cups sliced white mushrooms
- 2 cloves garlic, minced
- 2 (6-ounce) boneless, skinless chicken breasts, grilled or broiled
- 10 ounces large shrimp, peeled and deveined
- ¾ cup diced roasted tomatoes (see note)
- ½ pound medium elbow macaroni or fusilli pasta, cooked according to package directions
- 2 tablespoons chopped fresh parsley

1. **Make the three-cheese Alfredo sauce:** In a small saucepan, melt the butter over medium-low heat. Stir in the garlic and cook until softened.

2. Add the cream cheese and stir until it melts and is smooth and creamy. Gradually whisk in the milk, then stir in the mozzarella. When the moz-

zarella has melted, stir in the Parmesan and stir until it too has melted. Season with the salt and pepper and keep warm.

3. **Make the garlic bread crumb crust:** In a bowl, whisk together the melted butter and olive oil. Stir in the granulated garlic. Toss the bread crumbs and Parmesan with the butter and oil mixture, then set aside.

4. **Assemble and bake the dish:** Preheat the oven to 375°F.

5. In a large saucepan, heat the olive oil over medium heat. Add the mushrooms and cook until lightly browned. Stir in the garlic and sauté 1 minute more.

6. Cut the grilled chicken breasts into bite-size pieces and stir into the pan. Add the shrimp and roasted tomatoes.

7. Stir the Alfredo sauce and cooked pasta into the saucepan. Gently mix until all the ingredients are well blended.

8. Spoon the mixture into a 9 x 13-inch baking dish or casserole. Cover evenly with the garlic bread crumb crust and bake for 20 to 25 minutes, or until the crust is toasted and the sauce is bubbling and browned.

9. Sprinkle with the parsley before serving.

. . . .
Makes 2 servings
. . . .

Roasted tomatoes can be found in the canned vegetable aisle of most markets. To make your own, simply core and halve 2 medium plum tomatoes and brush the cut surfaces with olive oil and minced garlic. Lightly season them with salt and pepper, then roast in a 400°F oven until wilted and a bit charred on top. Let them cool completely and cut into smaller pieces.

DENNY'S
Biscuits & Gravy with Hash Browns

. . . .

DENNY'S OFFERS A NUMBER OF VALUE MENU BREAKFASTS, WHICH MIGHT SOUND
TEMPTING ON A BUSY MORNING. BUT NOTHING BEATS HOME-COOKED USING
YOUR OWN HEALTHY INGREDIENTS! THEIR $4 BISCUIT AND GRAVY BREAKFAST
COMES WITH HASH BROWNS AND EGGS.

. . . .

Pork Sausage Gravy

1 tablespoon unsalted butter
½ pound breakfast sausage,
   crumbled
3 tablespoons all-purpose flour

¼ teaspoon kosher salt
¼ teaspoon black pepper
Pinch of cayenne pepper
1¾ cups milk

Assembly

1 (16-ounce) can refrigerated
   large biscuits (8 biscuits)

1 pound store-bought hash
   brown potatoes, fresh or
   frozen

1. **Make the pork sausage gravy:** In a medium skillet, melt the butter.
   Add the crumbled sausage and cook, stirring frequently, until no longer
   pink in the center.

2. Sprinkle the sausage with the flour, salt, black pepper, and cayenne.
   Slowly simmer until the flour has been absorbed by the cooking liquid,
   about a minute.

3. Using a wooden spoon, gradually stir in the milk, scraping up any
   browned bits from the bottom of the skillet. Bring the mixture to a simmer and let it cook until thickened, stirring frequently. Taste the gravy
   and adjust the seasonings if desired and keep it warm.

4. **Assemble the dish:** Bake the biscuits according to the package directions.

5. Follow the instructions for making four 4-ounce servings of the hash
   brown potatoes.

6. For each serving, split 2 of the baked biscuits and arrange them on a dish split side up. Spoon some of the sausage gravy over each of the servings and add a portion of the hash brown potatoes to the plate. Serve hot.

Makes 4 servings

You may need to adjust portion sizes for smaller appetites. One biscuit, a tablespoon of gravy, and two tablespoons of potatoes should be enough to get a kid's day started right.

DENNY'S
Chocolate Chip Pancakes

DENNY'S HAS A "BUILD YOUR OWN PANCAKE" PROGRAM THAT LETS DINERS CHOOSE THE BATTER, MIX-INS, AND TOPPINGS FOR A SHORT OR TALL STACK. DON'T LET THE KIDS GO CRAZY—MAKE THESE CHOCOLATE CHIP "PUPPIES" FOR BREAKFAST AND THEY WON'T KNOW ANYTHING ELSE EXISTS!

1½ cups all-purpose flour
2 tablespoons sugar
3½ teaspoons baking powder
½ teaspoon kosher salt
1¼ cups milk
3 tablespoons unsalted butter, melted
2 tablespoons cold water

1 egg, well beaten
½ teaspoon vanilla extract
Cooking spray
½ cup semisweet or milk chocolate chips
Powdered sugar, maple syrup, or whipped cream, for serving

1. In a large bowl, whisk the flour, sugar, baking powder, and salt until well blended.

2. In a separate bowl, whisk together the milk, melted butter, water, egg, and vanilla. Whisk the milk mixture into the flour mixture and stir until very well blended and lump free.

3. Heat a skillet over medium heat and coat with cooking spray.

4. Pour ¼ cup of the batter for each pancake, less for the smaller "puppies." Sprinkle immediately with several of the chocolate chips and wait until holes bubble on the surface of the batter. Check to see if the bottoms of the pancakes have browned, then flip them over and brown the second side. Work in batches until all the batter has been used up.

5. Serve with powdered sugar, maple syrup, or whipped cream.

Makes 4 to 6 servings

Some other great mix-in ideas include fruits, such as blueberries or chopped bananas, chopped nuts, or cooked bacon bits.

DENNY'S
Jr Dippable Veggies

THIS IS A HEALTHY AFTER-SCHOOL OPTION IN PLACE OF SWEETS OR STARCHY SNACKS. BUYING PRECUT VEGETABLES SAVES TIME AND CAN STAVE OFF THE TEMPTATION TO FALL BACK ON PROCESSED FOODS.

1 (1-ounce) packet dry ranch dressing mix, such as Hidden Valley
1 cup milk
1 cup mayonnaise

2 ribs celery, cut into sticks
2 carrots, peeled and cut into sticks
1 small cucumber, peeled, seeded, and cut into sticks

1. In a bowl, whisk together the ranch dressing mix, milk, and mayonnaise. Cover and refrigerate until ready to serve.
2. Arrange the vegetables on a platter with the dressing for dipping.

Makes 2 or 3 servings

Bags of peeled and ready-to-eat baby carrots are widely available in markets. Keep a bag handy for when there's no time to peel and cut whole carrots.

DOMINO'S
Chocolate Lava Cake

YOU CAN ORDER THIS LUSCIOUS BELGIAN CHOCOLATE LAVA CAKE FROM DOMINO'S WHEN YOU ORDER PIZZA, BUT YOU CAN ALSO MAKE IT AT HOME TO RIP-ROARING REVIEWS.

Cooking spray
8 tablespoons (1 stick) unsalted butter
4 ounces semisweet chocolate chips
1 cup powdered sugar, sifted
1 tablespoon strong brewed coffee, chilled

1 teaspoon vanilla extract
¼ teaspoon ground cinnamon
2 whole eggs
1 egg yolk
6 tablespoons all-purpose flour
Ice cream, powdered sugar, or whipped cream, for serving

1. Preheat the oven to 425°F. Lightly coat four 4-ounce ramekins with cooking spray.

2. In the top of a double boiler, combine the butter and chocolate and stir over simmering water until melted.

3. Whisk in the powdered sugar. Stir in the cold coffee, vanilla, and cinnamon. Add the whole eggs, one at a time, beating thoroughly after each addition. Beat in the egg yolk.

4. Stir the flour into the batter, stirring constantly. Mix until the batter is smooth and thick.

5. Spoon a fourth of the batter into each of the prepared ramekins and set them on a baking sheet. Bake the cakes for 12 to 15 minutes, or until the surface of the cakes seems firm.

6. Invert the ramekins onto individual serving plates and carefully lift them off the baked cakes.

7. Just before serving, use a small spoon to poke a hole in the cake so that the "chocolate lava" comes pouring out.

8. Serve with ice cream, powdered sugar, or whipped cream.

Makes 4 servings

The stronger the coffee used in the recipe the richer it will be. Consider using espresso or twice-brewed regular coffee to add even more flavor.

DUNKIN' DONUTS
French Crullers

LIGHT AND AIRY, CRULLERS GET THEIR NAME FROM A DUTCH WORD THAT MEANS CURL, WHICH EXPLAINS THEIR TWISTED SHAPE. FOR THE BEST RESULTS, USE A STAND MIXER FITTED WITH THE PADDLE ATTACHMENT AND A PASTRY BAG FITTED WITH A ¾-INCH STAR TIP.

1 cup water	3 eggs
6 tablespoons unsalted butter	2 egg whites, lightly beaten
2 teaspoons superfine sugar	3 to 4 cups canola oil, for
¼ teaspoon fine sea salt	deep-frying
1 cup all-purpose flour, sifted	Cooking spray

Honey Glaze

1½ cups powdered sugar	3 to 4 tablespoons milk
1 tablespoon honey	

1. In a heavy-bottomed medium saucepan, bring the water, butter, sugar, and salt to a rolling boil.

2. Stir the flour in all at once, stirring constantly, until it is thoroughly incorporated. Keep stirring with a wooden spoon until a light glaze forms over the bottom of the saucepan and the batter begins to pull away from the sides of the pan.

3. Transfer the dough to the bowl of a stand mixer fitted with the paddle attachment to mix it slowly for 1 minute, cooling down the dough.

4. Increase the speed of the mixer to medium and beat in the eggs, one at a time, beating after each addition.

5. Add the beaten egg whites a little at a time and mix until the dough becomes smooth and glossy.

6. Fill a pastry bag (fitted with a ¾-inch star tip) with the dough and refrigerate it for 1 hour.

7. Fill a heavy-bottomed saucepan or electric fryer halfway with the vegetable oil and heat to 325F° (use a deep-fry thermometer).

8. Lightly coat a sheet of parchment paper with cooking spray. Pipe 3-inch rings onto the paper, arranging them about 2 inches apart. Set a wire rack over a baking sheet.

9. Working in batches, carefully place the crullers in the hot oil and fry them, flipping only once, until puffed up and golden brown, about 15 minutes. Use a slotted spoon to transfer the fried crullers to the wire rack. Let them cool completely.

10. **Make the honey glaze:** In a shallow bowl, thoroughly whisk together the powdered sugar, honey, and milk.

11. When the crullers are completely cool, dip the top of each one into the glaze and return it to the rack on the baking sheet.

12. When the glaze has set, the crullers are ready to serve.

Makes 12 servings

To save a few calories, you might want to try baking the doughnuts: Make the dough (steps 1 through 6). Preheat the oven to 450°F and line a baking sheet with parchment paper. Pipe the crullers directly onto the parchment paper, about 2 inches apart. Bake for 5 minutes, then reduce the oven temperature to 350°F and continue to bake for another 15 minutes. Turn off the oven, open the door just a crack, and let them sit for 5 to 10 minutes. When completely cool, dip in the glaze as described above.

FAMOUS DAVE'S
Banana Pudding

- -

NOTHING SAYS COMFORT FOOD LIKE BANANA PUDDING. FAMOUS DAVE'S MAKES
ONE OF THE BEST, AND NOW SO CAN YOU.

- -

6 medium size ripe bananas	4 tablespoons (½ stick) unsalted
4 cups milk	butter, cut into pieces
1½ cups sugar	2 teaspoons vanilla extract
⅔ cup all-purpose flour	Cooking spray
½ teaspoon kosher salt	1 (12-ounce) box vanilla wafers
5 egg yolks, well beaten	1 (8-ounce) container frozen
	whipped topping

1. Cut the bananas crosswise into ¼- to ½-inch-thick slices. Set aside.

2. In a large saucepan, whisk together the milk, sugar, flour, and salt over medium-low heat. Bring the mixture to a low boil and cook for 2 minutes, stirring constantly. The pudding will begin to thicken as the sugar dissolves.

3. Remove the pan from the heat and ladle ½ cup of the hot milk into the beaten egg yolks, whisking constantly. Whisk the warmed egg yolks back into the pan, stirring constantly, then stir over medium heat for about 3 minutes.

4. Remove the saucepan from the heat and stir in the butter and vanilla. Whisk until the butter is melted and well blended. Let the mixture cool for about 10 minutes.

5. Coat a 9 x 13-inch baking dish with cooking spray and arrange the vanilla wafers in a single layer over the bottom of the dish.

6. Cover the wafers with the sliced bananas and pour the pudding over the cookies and fruit, smoothing it over evenly with a spatula.

7. Refrigerate for at least 1 hour, or until completely chilled.

8. Spoon the whipped topping over the pudding and serve, or cover with plastic wrap and refrigerate until needed.

Makes 9 to 12 servings

The vanilla wafers will eventually get mushy if any leftover dessert sits for a while. Scoop up days-old pudding and mash it with a fork, set a few new crushed wafers in the bottom of a glass, and make a parfait dessert. Top it with a little more whipped topping, chopped nuts, and a maraschino cherry.

FATBURGER
Banana Shake

FILE THIS ONE IN THE GREATEST HITS SECTION OF YOUR RECIPE ORGANIZER. TRY CHOCOLATE OR LEMON PUDDING WITH YOUR FAVORITE ICE CREAM FOR VARIETY.

1 cup vanilla ice cream, slightly softened
¼ cup milk

2 teaspoons instant banana pudding powder
Whipped cream and nuts, for topping (optional)

1. In a blender, combine the ice cream, milk, and pudding powder and process until smooth and creamy.
2. Pour into a chilled glass and top with the whipped cream and nuts if desired.

Makes 1 serving

You can always use a ripe banana in place of the powder for a more nutritious shake. Cut off a few calories by using light ice cream and fat-free milk.

FIVE GUYS
Bacon Cheeseburger

THESE ARE HUMONGOUS DOUBLE BACON CHEESEBURGERS FROM FIVE GUYS. CUT THE SANDWICHES IN QUARTERS TO FEED THE YOUNGER CROWD, AND SERVE WITH COLESLAW OR CHIPS.

6 slices thick-cut bacon
1 tablespoon unsalted butter
8 ounces button mushrooms, stemmed and sliced
1 small yellow onion, chopped
1 pound lean ground chuck or sirloin
2 teaspoons kosher salt
½ teaspoon pepper

2 large hamburger buns, split
Condiments: Mayonnaise, ketchup, mustard, relish, steak sauce, or barbecue sauce
4 slices cheese, such as Cheddar, Monterey Jack, or American
Toppings: Lettuce, pickles, sliced tomatoes, jalapeños, green bell peppers

1. In a skillet, cook the bacon until crispy and drain on paper towels.

2. In a separate skillet, melt the butter over medium heat. Add the mushrooms and onion and cook until they are browned. Set aside and keep warm. Wipe out the skillet.

3. Form the ground beef into 4 patties and season them with salt and pepper.

4. Heat the same skillet or a griddle and cook the patties until seared on both sides and cooked to your preferred doneness.

5. To assemble the burgers, put the bottom half of each bun on a plate and spread with your choice of condiments, if using.

6. Put on one of the cooked patties, top it with a slice of cheese, then add another patty and slice of cheese. Top each burger with three strips of cooked bacon.

7. Spoon equal amounts of the mushroom and onion mixture over each burger, then add the toppings of your choice.

8. Finish with the top half of the bun and serve hot.

Makes 2 servings

These can easily be made into 4 single cheeseburgers, just add 2 more slices of bacon and 2 more hamburger buns.

FRIENDLY'S
Chicken Quesadillas

THESE ARE EASY TO MAKE AND ARE ALWAYS A HIT WITH KIDS. MAKE SURE YOU TURN THEM OVER HALFWAY THROUGH THE BAKING TIME SO THAT BOTH SIDES GET CRISPY.

1 pound chicken breast, diced
1 (1.27-ounce) packet fajita seasoning mix
Cooking spray
1 tablespoon olive oil
2 green bell peppers, chopped
2 red bell peppers, chopped
1 yellow onion, chopped

12 (10-inch) flour tortillas
4 slices bacon, crisp-cooked and crumbled
8 ounces Cheddar cheese, shredded
8 ounces Monterey Jack cheese, shredded

1. Preheat the broiler and line the broiler pan with foil.
2. Toss the diced chicken with the fajita seasoning until well coated and broil until cooked through and no longer pink in the center.
3. Preheat the oven to 375°F. Lightly coat a baking sheet with cooking spray or vegetable oil.
4. In a large skillet, heat the olive oil over medium heat. Add the bell peppers and onion and cook until softened and cooked through.
5. Layer half of each tortilla with the cooked chicken, sautéed vegetables, and bacon. Sprinkle the mixture with equal amounts of Cheddar and Jack cheeses.
6. Fold the empty side of the tortilla over and arrange the quesadillas on the prepared baking sheet.
7. Bake for 10 to 12 minutes, turning them over halfway through the cooking time, until the cheeses have melted and the tortillas are browned.
8. Serve whole as is, or cut each quesadilla in half before serving.

Makes 12 servings

Serve the quesadillas with fresh guacamole, salsa, and sour cream if desired.

GOLDEN CORRAL
Bread Pudding

KIDS FLOCK TO THE DESSERT SECTION OF GOLDEN CORRAL'S FAMOUS BUFFET. THIS BREAD PUDDING RECIPE WILL BE A HIT AT HOME AS WELL.

Pudding

Cooking spray or melted butter, for baking dish

2 cups milk

8 tablespoons (1 stick) unsalted butter, melted

½ cup packed dark brown sugar

1 teaspoon ground cinnamon

Pinch of kosher salt

2 eggs

3 cups cubed day-old French or sourdough bread, crusts removed

Vanilla Sauce

1 cup milk

2 tablespoons unsalted butter

1 tablespoon vanilla extract

½ cup granulated sugar

1 tablespoon all-purpose flour

¼ teaspoon kosher salt

1. **Make the pudding:** Preheat the oven to 350°F. Lightly coat a 7 x 11-inch baking dish with cooking spray or melted butter.

2. Heat a medium saucepan over high heat, then pour in the milk—it will scald on contact. Stir in the melted butter and set the pan aside to cool slightly.

3. In small bowl, whisk together the brown sugar, cinnamon, and salt. In a separate bowl, beat the eggs, then whisk in the brown sugar mixture.

4. When the milk mixture has cooled down, pour about ½ cup into the eggs, whisking constantly. When the mixture is well blended, whisk the warmed egg mixture into the saucepan, stirring constantly.

5. Toss in the bread cubes and stir to coat them evenly.

6. Pack the soaked bread cubes into the baking dish. Bake for about 40 minutes, or until the top is browned and slightly crispy and a toothpick

inserted into the center comes out clean. Set the dish aside while preparing the vanilla sauce.

7. **Make the vanilla sauce:** In a small saucepan, whisk together the milk, butter, vanilla, granulated sugar, flour, and salt. Bring to a boil and stir constantly, until the butter melts and the sauce has thickened, 3 to 4 minutes.

8. Reduce the heat to low and let the sauce simmer until the flour has cooked out, about 10 minutes. Let the sauce cool for about 5 minutes, then pour half of it over the bread pudding and serve the remaining sauce on the side.

9. Serve the pudding warm or at room temperature.

Makes 8 to 12 servings

Once the pudding is cooked, transfer to individual ramekins and add the vanilla sauce. Refrigerate the ramekins so they can be ready for an after-school snack or a nice-size dessert portion for kids.

GOLDEN CORRAL
Macaroni Salad

MACARONI SALAD GOES FROM PLAIN TO PERFECT AT THE GOLDEN CORRAL RES-
TAURANTS. THE SECRET IS MONTREAL SEASONING MIX, USUALLY USED ON STEAK.
YOU CAN GENERALLY FIND THIS MIXTURE IN THE SPICE AISLE AT MARKETS, OR
YOU CAN MAKE YOUR OWN LARGE BATCH (SEE RECIPE BELOW) AND KEEP IT ON
HAND FOR OTHER DISHES.

1 pound elbow macaroni, cooked
according to package directions
1 cup diced celery
1 cup diced red onion
1 cup shredded carrots
1 cup sweet pickle relish

2 cups mayonnaise
2 tablespoons lemon juice
1 tablespoon Montreal steak
seasoning, homemade (recipe
follows) or store-bought

1. In a large bowl, combine the cooked macaroni with the celery, onion, carrots, and relish.

2. In a small bowl, whisk together the mayonnaise, lemon juice, and Montreal seasoning.

3. Stir the dressing into the macaroni and vegetables, blending thoroughly.

4. Cover and chill until needed.

Makes 10 servings

Montreal Seasoning Mix

¼ cup kosher salt
1 tablespoon black peppercorns
1 tablespoon dried minced onion
1 tablespoon dried thyme

1 tablespoon dried rosemary
2 teaspoons fennel seeds
½ tablespoon granulated garlic
½ tablespoon red pepper flakes

In a small food processor or spice grinder, process all the ingredients until well ground. Store in a glass or plastic container with a tight-fitting lid.

Makes about ½ cup

GOLDEN CORRAL
Texas Toast

TEXAS TOAST IS TWICE THE THICKNESS OF REGULAR WHITE BREAD. CUT THE PIECES INTO HALVES OR QUARTERS FOR KIDS, OR EVEN JUST TO STRETCH THE SERVINGS.

Melted butter or olive oil, for the baking sheet
2 tablespoons unsalted butter, softened
4 slices Texas toast bread
½ teaspoon granulated garlic

1 cup shredded mozzarella cheese
2 green onions (white parts only), thinly sliced
1 teaspoon paprika

1. Preheat the oven to 400°F. Coat a baking sheet with a little melted butter or olive oil.
2. Spread the softened butter on one side of each slice of bread. Sprinkle each slice with the granulated garlic and mozzarella. Top with the green onions and paprika.
3. Put the bread on the baking sheet and toast in the hot oven for 5 minutes, or until the cheese is melted and the bottom side of the bread is golden.
4. Serve warm.

Makes 2 to 4 servings

IHOP
Blueberry Cheesecake Pancakes

LIGHT AND FLUFFY BLUEBERRY PANCAKES ARE ALWAYS DELICIOUS, AND THE STACKS AT IHOP ARE AT THE TOP OF EVERYONE'S LIST.

1 (4-ounce) package cream cheese, quartered and frozen
1 cup all-purpose flour
2 tablespoons sugar
1 teaspoon baking powder
½ teaspoon baking soda
¼ teaspoon kosher salt
1 egg

1 cup milk
2 tablespoons unsalted butter, melted
1 cup fresh or frozen blueberries
1 or 2 tablespoons butter, cut in pieces, for the griddle
Blueberry syrup, store-bought or homemade

1. Chop the frozen cream cheese into small pieces.

2. In a large bowl, whisk together the flour, sugar, baking powder, baking soda, and salt.

3. In a separate bowl, beat the egg well, then beat in the milk and melted butter. Stir to combine thoroughly.

4. Whisk the egg mixture into the flour mixture. Stir in the pieces of cream cheese. Mix in the blueberries. Set the batter aside for 10 minutes.

5. Heat a griddle or large skillet over medium heat and melt a small amount of butter.

6. Pour ¼ cup of the batter per pancake. Cook until bubbles rise to the surface of the batter and the bottom is golden brown. Flip the pancakes and cook until the second side is browned. Working in batches, use up all the batter.

7. Serve with blueberry syrup or maple syrup if preferred.

Makes 4 servings

Make smaller silver dollar pancakes for the kids. The pancakes are rich and filling, and the adult size might be a bit much. You can garnish this with a few fresh blueberries as well.

JAMBA JUICE
Blueberry Strawberry Blast-Off

FOR FEWER CALORIES AND A DIFFERENT TEXTURE, USE FAT-FREE MILK OR LOW-FAT YOGURT INSTEAD OF THE JUICE.

½ ripe banana, sliced
¾ cup blueberries, frozen and not thawed
¾ cup strawberries, frozen and not thawed

1 cup berry juice or V8 Berry Blend
1 cup ice cubes

1. In a blender, combine the banana, frozen berries, and berry juice and process until smooth.
2. Add the ice cubes and pulse until the ice is crushed uniformly—no big ice chunks should remain.
3. Serve immediately.

Makes 2 servings

I suggest using frozen fruit for convenience sake, but fresh is of course great. And this recipe is a fabulous way to use up anything overripe. Just blend with cubed or crushed ice.

JAMBA JUICE
Poppin' Peach Mango

A TRULY TROPICAL EXPERIENCE! THE MANGOES AND PASSION FRUIT JUICE CAN BE
FOUND IN THE FREEZER CASE OF LARGER MARKETS, AS WELL AS FRESH IN SEASON.

l cup sliced mangoes, frozen and
    not thawed
l cup sliced peaches, frozen and
    not thawed

l small ripe banana, sliced
l cup passion fruit juice
l cup ice cubes

1. In a blender, combine the mangoes, peaches, banana, and passion fruit
    juice and process until smooth.
2. Add the ice cubes and pulse until the ice is crushed uniformly—no big
    ice chunks should remain.
3. Serve immediately.

Makes 2 servings

*Passion fruit juice is often mixed with other fruits, such as
mango and guava. Use a blend if you can't find the juice on its
own.*

JAMBA JUICE
Strawberries Gone Bananas

BANANAS AND BERRIES ARE A CLASSIC COMBINATION. MAKE THIS SMOOTHIE WITH
A JUICE MADE FROM A BLEND OF BERRIES.

1 ripe banana, chopped
¾ cup strawberries, frozen and
   not thawed
¾ cup strawberry sherbet

½ cup strawberry yogurt, regular
   or nonfat
1 cup berry juice, plus more as
   needed
1 cup ice cubes

1. In a blender, combine the banana, strawberries, sherbet, yogurt, and
   juice.
2. Add the ice cubes and pulse until the ice is crushed uniformly—no big
   ice chunks should remain.
3. Serve immediately.

Makes 2 servings

*If using a sugar-free or reduced-sugar juice, be sure to use
100% fruit juice with no added sugar.*

JOE'S CRAB SHACK
Crab Cakes

JOE'S CRAB CAKES ARE CRUNCHY ON THE OUTSIDE AND CREAMY ON THE INSIDE. THESE ARE VERY SIMPLE TO PREPARE AND CAN BE MADE ANY SIZE YOU WANT, FROM TINY BITE-SIZE BALLS FOR APPETIZERS TO LARGER ENTRÉE SIZES.

1 egg
¼ cup mayonnaise
¼ cup chopped fresh parsley
1 tablespoon Worcestershire sauce
1 teaspoon lemon juice
1 teaspoon dry mustard
1 teaspoon black pepper
½ teaspoon Old Bay seasoning
½ teaspoon kosher salt
¼ teaspoon red pepper flakes
½ cup unseasoned dried bread crumbs
1 pound crabmeat (Dungeness, blue, or jumbo lump crabmeat in a can), thawed and well drained if frozen
½ cup all-purpose flour
3 cups canola oil, for deep-frying

1. In a large bowl, beat the egg. Add the mayonnaise, parsley, Worcestershire sauce, lemon juice, mustard, black pepper, Old Bay, salt, and pepper flakes and combine all the ingredients.

2. Fold in the bread crumbs, then gently mix in the crabmeat.

3. Form the mixture into 6 crab cakes (using a 3- or 4-inch ring mold will help you make perfect cakes) and coat them lightly with the flour.

4. In a heavy-bottomed saucepan or electric fryer, heat the oil to 375°F (use a deep-fry thermometer).

5. Deep-fry the cakes, turning only once, until they are golden on each side.

6. Drain on paper towels or a wire rack, then serve hot.

Makes 6 servings

Serve the crab cakes with your favorite seafood sauce. Good choices would be tartar, cocktail, creamy horseradish, or a garlic aioli like the one Joe's serves with this dish.

JOE'S CRAB SHACK
Pastalaya

THIS IS JOE'S COMBINATION OF PASTA AND JAMBALAYA, EASY TO SERVE IN SMALL OR LARGE PORTIONS. BE SURE TO CUT THE ANDOUILLE SAUSAGE INTO SMALLER THAN BITE-SIZE PIECES.

2 tablespoons olive or canola oil
½ cup andouille sausage, halved lengthwise and cut crosswise into ½-inch pieces
4 tablespoons (½ stick) unsalted butter
1 cup chopped yellow onion
2 large cloves garlic, minced
1 tablespoon Cajun seasoning, store-bought or homemade
½ cup red bell pepper squares (1-inch)

½ cup yellow bell pepper squares (1-inch)
½ cup green bell pepper squares (1-inch)
1 cup quartered stemmed mushrooms
⅓ cup chicken broth, warmed
1 pound small shrimp, peeled, deveined, and tails removed
2 cups penne, cooked according to package directions
½ cup shredded fresh basil
¼ cup grated Parmesan cheese

1. In a large skillet, heat the oil over medium heat. Add the sausage and cook for a couple of minutes, or until lightly browned. Remove with a slotted spoon and drain on paper towels. Wipe out the skillet.

2. Add the butter to the skillet and melt over medium heat. Add the onion and garlic and cook until limp. Sprinkle with the Cajun seasoning.

3. Stir in the bell peppers and mushrooms and stir frequently for about 5 minutes, or until cooked through. Add the chicken broth and shrimp and simmer over lower heat just until the shrimp are cooked through.

4. Toss the cooked penne with the mixture and add the cooked sausage. When they have warmed through, stir in the shredded basil.

5. Sprinkle with the Parmesan just before serving.

Makes 6 servings

If making this recipe for kids, the flavors may be a bit too pronounced. Cut back on the Cajun seasoning if kids are not used to it.

JOE'S CRAB SHACK
Shrimp Alfredo

JOE'S MAKES ALL THEIR SAUCES AND SOUPS FROM SCRATCH, BUT YOU CAN SAVE
YOURSELF SOME TIME BY USING QUALITY PREPARED PRODUCTS. FOR THE ALFREDO
SAUCE IN THIS RECIPE, TRY A JAR FROM EMERIL LAGASSE OR CLASSICO.

4 tablespoons (½ stick) unsalted
butter

2 tablespoons extra virgin olive oil

1 cup diced yellow onion

2 large cloves garlic, minced

¾ cup diced red bell pepper

1 cup diced portobello
mushrooms

1 pound medium shrimp, peeled
and deveined

1 (15-ounce) jar Alfredo sauce,
store-bought or homemade

½ cup grated Romano cheese

½ cup heavy (whipping) cream

¼ teaspoon cayenne pepper

Kosher salt and black pepper

12 ounces penne, cooked
according to package directions

¼ cup chopped fresh parsley

1. In a large saucepan, heat the butter and olive oil over medium heat. Stir
    in the onion and garlic and cook until they are translucent and soft,
    about 2 minutes. Stir in the red bell pepper and mushrooms and cook,
    stirring frequently, for about 2 minutes.

2. Add the shrimp to the pan and cook just until they are firm and just
    cooked through.

3. Stir in the Alfredo sauce, Romano, and heavy cream. Just heat the sauce
    through, don't let it boil. Season the sauce with the cayenne, then adjust
    with salt and black pepper.

4. Toss the penne with the finished sauce and sprinkle with the chopped
    parsley just before serving.

Makes 6 servings

*Add some fresh veggies to this dish! Tomatoes, cauliflower, peas,
and string beans would go well—and be a clever way to sneak
vegetables onto kids' plates.*

JOHNNY CARINO'S
Chicken Scaloppini

JOHNNY CARINO'S SERVES THIS CHICKEN DISH OVER A MOUND OF SPAGHETTI SMOTHERED IN LEMON BUTTER SAUCE AND CREAM. CUT THE SERVING SIZES IN HALF FOR YOUNGER FAMILY MEMBERS, AS THE RICHNESS OF THE DISH WILL LEAVE NO ROOM FOR ANYTHING ELSE. PREPARE THE LEMON BUTTER AHEAD OF TIME SO IT HAS TIME TO FIRM UP.

Lemon Butter
2 sticks (½ pound) unsalted
   butter, softened
1 tablespoon lemon juice

2 tablespoons dry white wine
1 clove garlic, minced

Chicken and Pasta
2 (6-ounce) boneless, skinless
   chicken breasts
4 tablespoons (½ stick) unsalted
   butter
2 Roma (plum) tomatoes, diced
½ cup sliced mushrooms
¾ cup chopped bacon, crisp-
   cooked

1 teaspoon granulated garlic
1 teaspoon kosher salt
1 teaspoon pepper
1 cup heavy (whipping) cream
½ pound spaghetti, cooked
   according to package directions

1. **Make the lemon butter:** In a bowl, with an electric mixer, beat together the softened butter, lemon juice, wine, and garlic. Beat at low speed until the butter is smooth and well combined. Scrape the butter into a small glass container with a tight-fitting lid and refrigerate until needed.

2. **Make the chicken and pasta:** Butterfly the chicken breasts. Pound the split pieces between sheets of plastic wrap so that they are of even thickness.

3. In a large skillet, melt the butter over medium heat. Add the pounded chicken breasts and cook, turning once, until no longer pink in the center. Remove the chicken and keep warm.

4. Stir the tomatoes, mushrooms, cooked bacon, granulated garlic, salt, and pepper into the skillet. Sauté the vegetables until cooked through and the tomatoes are starting to fall apart.

5. Chop the hardened lemon butter in chunks. Stir the heavy cream into the skillet and bring to a boil. Reduce the heat and whisk in the lemon butter. When all the pieces have been incorporated, add the spaghetti and toss to evenly coat it with the sauce.

6. Return the chicken breasts to the pan and let them heat through.

7. To serve, place a portion of spaghetti on each plate and top with 2 pieces of chicken. Pour the remaining sauce over the chicken and pasta.

Makes 2 servings

This dish may be easier for smaller kids to deal with if the chicken is cut into bite-size pieces either before cooking or before serving. If spaghetti is too much for their little hands to handle, consider using penne or fusilli.

JOHNNY CARINO'S
Chicken Balsamico

BALSAMIC VINEGAR ADDS A TOUCH OF SWEETNESS AND DEPTH TO THIS PASTA
DISH. THE SPINACH TOSSED IN IS NOT ONLY COLORFUL BUT ALSO A GREAT SOURCE
OF NUTRITION FOR PICKY VEGETABLE EATERS!

4 (8-ounce) boneless, skinless
  chicken breasts
Kosher salt and pepper

½ cup all-purpose flour
3 tablespoons olive oil
½ cup balsamic vinegar

Tomatoes and Spinach
2 tablespoons olive oil
2 large cloves garlic, minced
12 ounces baby spinach
1 cup diced (½-inch) Roma
  (plum) tomatoes

Kosher salt and pepper
10 ounces angel hair pasta,
  cooked according to package
  directions
¼ cup grated Parmesan cheese

1. Butterfly the chicken breasts in half so you will end up with 2 pieces, called medallions, per serving.

2. Season the chicken with salt and pepper, then dust them lightly in the flour.

3. In a large skillet, heat the olive oil over medium heat. Working in batches if necessary, add the chicken and cook, turning once, until cooked through and no longer pink in the center.

4. Return all of the chicken to the pan, add the balsamic vinegar, and let simmer until almost completely reduced. Turn the pieces of chicken so they are coated with the vinegar as it cooks down.

5. **Meanwhile, prepare the tomatoes and spinach:** In a separate skillet, heat the olive oil over medium heat. Add the garlic and cook, stirring frequently, until it is softened.

6. Add the spinach and let it cook down. When the liquid released by the spinach is evaporated, add the diced tomatoes. Season the vegetables with salt and pepper. Toss the cooked spaghetti with the spinach and tomatoes.

7. To serve, place a portion of spaghetti on each of 4 plates. Shingle the chicken medallions over the pasta and spinach and drizzle with any remaining pan juices. Sprinkle with the Parmesan.

Makes 4 servings

This is another recipe that can be adjusted for smaller hands. Break the dry angel hair into pieces before cooking to make it more manageable and cut the chicken into short strips.

KFC
Crispy Potato Wedges

THESE WELL-SEASONED POTATOES ARE JUST THE THING TO GO WITH A HEARTY
MEAL OF MEATLOAF OR GRILLED SALMON. THEY ALSO MAKE A GREAT GARNISH FOR
SALADS AND SANDWICHES.

3 to 4 cups canola oil, for
  deep-frying
I cup milk
I egg, well beaten
I cup all-purpose flour
I ½ tablespoons kosher salt
I teaspoon pepper

½ teaspoon seasoned salt, such
  as Lawry's
¼ teaspoon paprika
½ teaspoon granulated garlic
5 russet (baking) potatoes, halved
  lengthwise then quartered into
  lengthwise wedges

1. In a heavy-bottomed saucepan or electric fryer, fill halfway with the oil
    and heat to 375°F (use a deep-fry thermometer).

2. In a shallow bowl, whisk together the milk and beaten egg until well
    combined. In a second bowl, whisk together the flour, kosher salt, pep-
    per, seasoned salt, paprika, and garlic.

3. Dip a few potato wedges at a time in the egg wash, then toss them or roll
    them in the seasoned flour.

4. Working in batches, fry the potatoes in the hot oil for 3 minutes. Drain
    on a wire rack while you cook the remaining potatoes.

5. After they are cooked once, return the wedges to the hot oil, and this
    time let them cook for 5 minutes. Check one wedge and make sure it is
    cooked through. Work in batches again and transfer them to the rack as
    they're done.

6. Serve hot.

Makes 4 to 6 servings

Cooking the potatoes twice crisps the outer surface, forming a seal that lets the wedges steam in the center. The potatoes continue to cook a bit while they are waiting for their second round of frying, then finish during the second frying period. If all this frying does not appeal to you, toss the seasoned wedges with a little olive oil or coat them with cooking spray and oven-roast them in a single layer at 400°F until done.

KRISPY KREME
Cookies and Cream Doughnuts

YOU WILL NEED A DOUGHNUT PAN OR TWO TO MAKE THESE BAKED TREATS, BUT THE NUMBER OF CALORIES SAVED BY NOT FRYING THEM WILL MAKE THE PURCHASE WORTHWHILE. A PASTRY BAG WILL MAKE FILLING THE DOUGHNUT PANS EASIER AND NEATER.

Doughnuts
Butter or cooking spray, for the pan
2 cups all-purpose flour
½ cup unsweetened cocoa powder
I teaspoon baking powder
½ teaspoon baking soda
½ teaspoon salt
½ cup granulated sugar
½ cup packed golden brown sugar
⅓ cup canola oil
2 eggs, well beaten
1½ teaspoons vanilla extract
¾ cup buttermilk

Oreo Whipped Cream
I cup heavy (whipping) cream
3 tablespoons powdered sugar
2 Oreo cookies, crushed

Oreo Vanilla Icing
3¾ cups powdered sugar
¼ cup milk, plus more as needed
I tablespoon heavy (whipping) cream
I teaspoon vanilla extract
8 Oreo cookies, crushed

1. **Make the doughnuts:** Preheat the oven to 350°F. Coat a doughnut pan with butter or cooking spray.

2. In a large bowl, whisk together the flour, cocoa powder, baking powder, baking soda, and salt. Make a well in the center of the mixture.

3. In a separate bowl, whisk together the granulated and brown sugars, oil, eggs, vanilla, and buttermilk until smooth and creamy. Pour the but-

termilk mixture into the well in the center of the flour mixture and use a wooden spoon to gradually incorporate the wet into the dry ingredients.

4. Fill a large pastry bag with the batter and pipe the mixture into the prepared doughnut pans until they are three-fourths full.

5. Bake for 12 to 13 minutes, or until a toothpick inserted in the center of a doughnut comes out clean.

6. Invert the doughnuts onto a wire rack and let them cool completely before icing and filling.

7. **Make the Oreo whipped cream:** In a bowl, with an electric mixer, whip the cream until soft peaks form. Beat in the powdered sugar, then increase the speed and whip the cream to stiff peaks. Fold in the crushed Oreos. Fill a pastry bag with the whipped cream.

8. **Make the Oreo vanilla icing:** In a medium bowl, whisk together the powdered sugar, milk, heavy cream, and vanilla. Add a little extra milk if the icing is too thick—it should be the consistency of a thick glaze.

9. To frost the doughnuts, use a spoon or pastry brush to coat the doughnuts with the icing. Sprinkle them immediately with the crushed Oreos.

10. Let the icing set, then pipe the whipped cream into the centers of the doughnuts.

11. Serve immediately or refrigerate in an airtight container.

Makes 12 servings

Doughnut pans are available from large stores such as Target and Macy's as well as from online retailers.

KRISPY KREME
Glazed Doughnuts

Doughnuts

3 envelopes (6.75 teaspoons)
quick-rising yeast

½ cup very warm water (about
110°F)

2¼ cups milk

¾ cup sugar

1½ teaspoons kosher salt

3 eggs, well beaten

½ cup vegetable shortening

7½ cups all-purpose flour, plus
more for rolling

2 to 3 cups canola oil, for
deep-frying

Doughnut Glaze

8 tablespoons (1 stick) unsalted
butter

3 cups powdered sugar, sifted

½ teaspoon vanilla extract

½ cup evaporated milk

1. **Make the doughnuts:** Stir the yeast into the warm water and let it sit for about 5 minutes.

2. Heat a medium saucepan over high heat, then pour in the milk—it will scald on contact. Remove the pan from the heat and let the milk cool.

3. In a bowl, with an electric mixer, whisk together the yeast mixture, the cooled milk, sugar, salt, eggs, and shortening. Mix just until combined, about 30 seconds.

4. Stir in 3 cups of the flour and beat on medium speed for about 2 minutes, scraping the sides of the bowl as needed. Add the remaining flour and mix just until blended—the batter does not need to be smooth.

5. Cover the bowl with a clean kitchen towel and let it sit in a draft-free area until it doubles in size, 30 minutes to 1 hour.

6. Flour a work surface and turn out the risen dough. Roll it around to coat it with the flour. Roll out the dough to about a ½-inch thickness. Cut into doughnuts with a doughnut cutter (which will give you the bonus of doughnut holes) or a round cookie or biscuit cutter. Re-roll the scraps to get more.

7. Cover the doughnuts with the kitchen towel and let them rise again before frying.

8. In a heavy-bottomed saucepan or electric fryer, heat the oil to 350°F (use a deep-fry thermometer).

9. Working in batches, carefully fry the doughnuts, turning only once until golden on both sides. You can use two spoons or chopsticks to turn them over, but be very careful not to puncture the surface of the doughnuts as that will allow the oil to seep inside.

10. Remove the doughnuts with a slotted spoon or skimmer to a wire rack to cool slightly.

11. **Meanwhile, make the glaze:** In a small saucepan, melt the butter over low heat. Whisk in the powdered sugar and vanilla. Stir until smooth and lump free. Add the evaporated milk a little at a time until the desired consistency is reached.

12. To finish the doughnuts, dip the top of each doughnut into the glaze and set it again on the wire rack to harden. Serve warm or at room temperature.

* * * * * * * * * *
Makes 3 dozen doughnuts
* * * * * * * * * *

Any scraps of dough can be rolled very thinly and cut into 3-inch rectangles with a wavy-edged ravioli cutter. Twist the dough strips once in the center and fry until crispy. Shower with powdered sugar or honey for an Italian-style fried pastry.

LOFTHOUSE
Chocolate Cookies

LOFTHOUSE IS A BAKING COMPANY HEADQUARTERED IN UTAH THAT SUPPLIES A WIDE VARIETY OF COOKIES NATIONWIDE. AVAILABLE AT MAJOR SUPERMARKET CHAINS, THEY ARE EASY TO DUPLICATE AT HOME.

Cookies

6 cups all-purpose flour, plus more for rolling out the dough

¾ cup unsweetened cocoa powder, plus more for rolling out the dough

1 teaspoon baking soda

1 teaspoon baking powder

½ teaspoon fine sea salt

8 tablespoons (1 stick) unsalted butter, softened

2 cups granulated sugar

3 eggs

1 teaspoon vanilla extract

1½ cups sour cream

Chocolate Butter Frosting

2 sticks (½ pound) unsalted butter, softened

1 teaspoon vanilla extract

1¼ cups powdered sugar

3 tablespoons unsweetened cocoa powder

¼ cup heavy (whipping) cream

1. **Make the cookies:** In a large bowl, whisk together 5 cups of the flour, the cocoa, baking soda, baking powder, and sea salt.

2. In a bowl, with an electric mixer, beat the butter and granulated sugar until light and creamy. Add the eggs, one at a time, beating after each addition. Beat in the vanilla and sour cream.

3. With the mixer on low speed, gradually beat in the flour mixture. The dough should be pliable and easy to roll out, so add the remaining 1 cup flour a little at a time until it reaches that consistency. Add a little extra if necessary, but don't let it get too stiff.

4. Divide the dough into 2 portions, wrap them in plastic wrap, and refrigerate overnight, or at least 6 hours.

5. Preheat the oven to 425°F. Line your largest baking sheets with parchment paper or silicone baking mats.

6. Dust a work surface with a combination of flour and cocoa powder.

7. Roll out the refrigerated dough to a ³/₄-inch thickness. Cut out cookies with a 2½-inch round cutter or the floured rim of a drinking glass. Re-roll the scraps to cut out more cookies. Transfer the cookies to the prepared baking sheets, placing them at least 2 inches apart.

8. Bake for 7 to 8 minutes, just until set, then transfer them to a wire rack to cool completely before frosting. The unfrosted cookies can be stored in a tightly covered container for up to 5 days.

9. **Make the chocolate butter frosting:** In a bowl, with an electric mixer, beat the butter and vanilla until light and fluffy. Beat in the powdered sugar and cocoa powder until well blended.

10. Add the heavy cream a spoonful at a time, until you reach a frosting consistency. You may add more cream if needed.

11. Spread the frosting over the cookies using a small spoon or metal spatula.

Makes 4 dozen cookies

Finish off these delicious treats with rainbow and chocolate sprinkles!

LOFTHOUSE
Soft Peanut Butter Chip Sugar Cookies

LOFTHOUSE IS KNOWN FOR ITS SOFT COOKIES, AND THESE ARE OOEY GOOEY, MELT-IN-YOUR-MOUTH TENDER. THIS RECIPE MAKES A SMALL BATCH, WHICH IS A GOOD THING SINCE THEY ARE SO ADDICTIVE!

Cookies
1¾ cups cake flour
2 teaspoons cornstarch
¼ teaspoon baking powder
¼ teaspoon baking soda
¼ teaspoon fine sea salt
8 tablespoons (1 stick) unsalted butter, softened

½ cup granulated sugar
½ cup packed light brown sugar
1 egg
2 teaspoons vanilla extract
10 ounces peanut butter chips

Peanut Butter Frosting
4 tablespoons (½ stick) unsalted butter, softened
⅓ cup creamy peanut butter

1½ cups powdered sugar
1 to 2 tablespoons milk, if needed

1. **Make the cookies:** In a bowl, whisk together the cake flour, cornstarch, baking powder, baking soda, and salt.

2. In a separate bowl, beat the butter with both the sugars until light and fluffy. Beat in the egg, then add the vanilla. Stir in the peanut butter chips.

3. Stir the flour mixture into the sugar mixture with a wooden spoon just until blended. Do not overmix this dough.

4. Using a 2-inch ice cream scoop or a tablespoon, drop 12 heaping mounds on a flat plate or baking sheet, then flatten them slightly.

5. Cover the plate with plastic wrap and refrigerate the cookies for at least 6 hours.

6. Preheat the oven to 350°F. Line a baking sheet with parchment paper or a silicone baking mat.

7. Place the refrigerated cookies on the prepared pan at least 2 inches apart. Bake for 8 to 9 minutes, or just until set. Let them cool on the baking sheet, then when firm enough, transfer them to a wire rack to cool completely before frosting. The unfrosted cookies can be stored in a tightly covered container for up to 5 days.

8. **Make the frosting:** In a bowl, with an electric mixer, cream the butter and peanut butter until light and fluffy. On medium speed, slowly beat in the powdered sugar. Add a few tablespoons of milk if the frosting is not a spreadable consistency.

9. Spread the frosting on the cookies with a small spoon or metal spatula. Decorate the cookies with chocolate sprinkles.

Makes 12 cookies

Increase the yield of this recipe by making smaller cookies—you should easily be able to get two dozen cookies by cutting down on the size.

LOFTHOUSE
Sugar Cookies

THESE SUGAR COOKIES HAVE JUST THE RIGHT AMOUNT OF SWEETNESS AND ARE
ENTICINGLY SOFT. AS GOOD AS THEY ARE LEFT PLAIN, THE BUTTERCREAM FROST-
ING TURNS THEM INTO A VERY SPECIAL TREAT.

Cookies

3½ cups all-purpose flour, plus
  more for rolling out the dough

½ teaspoon baking soda

½ teaspoon baking powder

½ teaspoon fine sea salt

1½ cups granulated sugar

8 tablespoons (1 stick) unsalted
  butter, softened

2 eggs

1 teaspoon vanilla extract

½ cup sour cream

2 ounces cream cheese, softened

Buttercream Frosting

8 tablespoons (1 stick) unsalted
  butter, softened

1 teaspoon vanilla extract

2½ cups powdered sugar

¼ cup milk

¼ cup multicolor sprinkles

1. **Make the cookies:** In a medium bowl, whisk together the flour, baking soda, baking powder, and salt.

2. In a separate bowl, with an electric mixer, beat the granulated sugar and butter until light and fluffy. Beat in the eggs, one at a time, beating after each addition. Beat in the vanilla, sour cream, and cream cheese, beating until well blended.

3. Slowly beat in the flour mixture, beating just until combined. The dough should feel sticky but firm. You may need to add a couple spoonfuls of flour to bring it to the proper consistency.

4. Put a large sheet of plastic wrap on a work surface. Scrape the dough onto the plastic and fold over the edges. Lightly smash the dough into a disk, then refrigerate for at least 6 hours.

5. Preheat the oven to 425°F. Line one or two baking sheets with parchment paper or silicone baking mats.

6. Flour a work surface and roll out the dough to a ¼-inch thickness. Cut out cookies with a 2½-inch round cookie cutter or the floured rim of a drinking glass. Re-roll scraps to cut out more cookies.

7. Place the cookies on the prepared baking sheets, placing them at least 2 inches apart. Bake for 6 to 7 minutes, or until they are just beginning to brown at the edges. Remove them to a wire rack to cool before frosting. The unfrosted cookies can be stored in an airtight container for up to 5 days.

8. **Make the buttercream frosting:** In a bowl, with an electric mixer, cream the butter until light and fluffy. Beat in the vanilla. With the mixer on low speed, gradually beat in the powdered sugar until it is well blended. Increase the speed to high and cream it a bit longer.

9. Stir in the milk, spoon by spoon, until the mixture reaches the proper consistency. Turn the mixer on high for a few seconds to make the frosting fluffy again.

10. Frost the cookies using a small spoon or a metal spatula and finish them off with the sprinkles.

Makes about 1½ dozen cookies

The dough can be prepared days ahead of time, tightly wrapped and refrigerated. You may find that the flavors are actually enhanced by the longer resting time.

MCDONALD'S
Chicken McNuggets

THIS IS A KID'S FAVORITE FOR SURE. WHEN WE MAKE IT AT HOME MY SON RYAN CAN'T GET ENOUGH OF THEM. HE PREFERS A BARBECUE SAUCE FOR DIPPING.

2 pounds boneless, skinless
  chicken breast
4 teaspoons kosher salt
½ teaspoon parsley flakes
½ teaspoon oregano

¼ teaspoon pepper
2 eggs
1 cup flour
2 cups corn oil

1. Cube chicken and place in a food processor. Add 2 teaspoons salt, the parsley, oregano, and pepper, and combine well. Blend chicken until it's a fine paste.
2. Beat eggs in a small bowl, set aside.
3. Combine the remaining 2 teaspoons salt and the flour on a large plate.
4. Roll the chicken paste into about 30 balls the size of golf balls.
5. Dip and immerse each chicken ball in the flour, then in the egg mix, and then in the flour again. Once the flour sticks and covers the chicken balls, flatten them down into nuggets 2 inches wide and 2 inches tall and set aside.
6. Fill a heavy-bottomed saucepan or electric fryer halfway with the oil and heat to 375°F (use a deep-fry thermometer)
7. Working in batches, fry the nuggets for about 6 to 8 minutes or until golden brown on both sides. Remove the nuggets to a towel-lined plate to catch the excess oil. Let them cool a bit, and serve.

Makes 6 servings

A deep-fry/candy thermometer or instant-read thermometer will help you maintain the correct temperature for frying. The temperature might drop between batches, so hold off frying the nuggets until it gets back to 375°F.

MCDONALD'S
Fruit and Maple Oatmeal

MCDONALD'S OFFERS A FAIRLY HEALTHY BREAKFAST CHOICE WITH THIS NOURISH-
ING OATMEAL. SERVE THE COOKED OATMEAL IN A 12-OUNCE PLASTIC CONTAINER,
WITH A LITTLE MILK AND CINNAMON, AND LET THE YOUNGSTERS TAKE IT TO GO.

⅔ cup water
⅓ cup rolled oats
¼ cup diced red apple
¼ cup diced green apple
1 tablespoon dried cranberries
1 tablespoon California raisins

1 tablespoon golden raisins
1 teaspoon real maple syrup
1 teaspoon molasses
1 teaspoon dark brown sugar
¼ teaspoon kosher salt
¼ cup milk, or more if desired

1. In a small saucepan, bring the water to a boil and stir in the oats. Reduce the heat and let the cereal simmer for a minute.

2. Stir in the apples, cranberries, raisins, maple syrup, molasses, brown sugar, and salt. Add a little extra water or milk if you like a thinner consistency.

3. Transfer the cereal to a bowl and top with the milk.

Makes 1 serving

*If there's no time in your hectic morning schedule to measure
and dice fresh fruit, double or triple the amount of dried
cranberries and raisins, and add dried apple pieces.*

THE MELTING POT
Spinach Artichoke Cheese Fondue

THE MELTING POT FEATURES AN ALL-FONDUE MENU. ONE OF THE MOST POPULAR
IS THIS CREAMY VEGETABLE FONDUE SERVED WITH PIECES OF FRENCH BREAD. IT
INCLUDES BUTTERKÄSE, WHICH IS A GERMAN BUTTER CHEESE THAT CAN BE HARD
TO FIND. SUBSTITUTE WITH SWISS CHEESE IF THE BUTTERKÄSE IS UNAVAILABLE.

½ cup vegetable broth
1 cup chopped spinach leaves
½ cup chopped artichoke hearts
3 cloves garlic, minced
½ cup shredded Butterkäse or
  Swiss cheese

½ cup shredded fontina cheese
2 tablespoons all-purpose flour
2 tablespoons grated Parmesan
  cheese
½ teaspoon Tabasco sauce
1 baguette

1. In a medium saucepan, heat the vegetable broth. Before it boils, add the
    spinach, artichoke hearts, and garlic. Simmer until the spinach is cooked
    down, stirring frequently.

2. In a bowl, toss the Butterkäse and fontina with the flour. Add the mix-
    ture a little at a time to the simmering vegetables and broth. When the
    first addition is melted, stir in the next, and so on until all the cheese has
    been melted into the vegetables.

3. When the fondue has reached a creamy consistency, stir in the Parmesan
    and Tabasco sauce.

4. Cut up the French bread or baguette into bite-size pieces and use forks
    to dip the bread into the fondue. Serve hot.

Makes 2 to 4 servings

*If you have a fondue set, transfer the melted cheese and
vegetables to the fondue pot and use the long prongs to dip the
bread into the fondue.*

OLD SPAGHETTI FACTORY
Spaghetti with Meat Sauce

THE SIMPLICITY OF THIS RECIPE WILL BE WELCOME ON A BUSY WEEKNIGHT. IF STRINGY SPAGHETTI IS TOO MESSY FOR YOUR LITTLE ONES, SUBSTITUTE A PASTA SHAPE THAT'S MORE SPOON FRIENDLY, SUCH AS SHELLS, BOW-TIES, OR ELBOW MACARONI.

1 tablespoon olive oil
2 yellow onions, chopped
2 cloves garlic, minced
2 pounds lean ground chuck or sirloin
1 tablespoon Italian seasoning
1 teaspoon kosher salt

½ teaspoon pepper
1 tablespoon granulated garlic
1 (28-ounce) can stewed tomatoes
2 (6-ounce) cans tomato paste
1 cup dry red wine or water
1 pound spaghetti, cooked according to package directions

1. In a large skillet, heat the oil over medium heat. Add the onions and garlic and cook until softened.

2. Crumble the ground beef and stir it into the onions. Let the beef cook until the liquid evaporates and the meat starts to brown, stirring frequently.

3. Season the meat with the Italian seasoning, salt, pepper, and granulated garlic.

4. Add the stewed tomatoes and tomato paste. Stir the mixture well and let it simmer over low heat for at least 1 hour. Add the red wine or water if the sauce gets too thick.

5. Warm the cooked pasta and divide it among heated shallow bowls. Top with the meat sauce and serve hot.

Makes 6 to 8 servings

Freshly chopped herbs will brighten the flavors of this dish. Try shredded basil, oregano, or parsley. The sauce gains depth when aged—make it a day or two before you need it and keep it covered in the refrigerator. Well-sealed in an airtight container, it can be frozen for a month.

OLIVE GARDEN
Five-Cheese Ziti Al Forno

THIS IS ONE OF THOSE GOOEY, RICH BAKED PASTA DISHES THAT OLIVE GARDEN IS FAMOUS FOR.

Ziti Sauce

4 cups tomato sauce, store-bought or homemade

2 cups Alfredo sauce, store-bought or homemade

½ cup ricotta cheese

¼ cup shredded mozzarella cheese

¼ cup shredded fontina cheese

1 teaspoon Italian seasoning

½ teaspoon pepper

Cheese Topping

3 cups shredded mozzarella cheese

¼ cup grated Romano cheese

¼ cup grated Parmesan cheese

½ cup dried Italian bread crumbs

2 cloves garlic, minced

2 tablespoons olive oil

¼ cup chopped fresh flat-leaf parsley

Ziti

Cooking spray or olive oil, for the baking dish

1 pound ziti pasta, cooked according to package directions

1 cup shredded mozzarella cheese

1. **Make the ziti sauce:** In a bowl, whisk together the tomato sauce and Alfredo sauce. When well combined, stir in the ricotta, mozzarella, and fontina. Season the mixture with the Italian seasoning and pepper. Set aside.

2. **Make the cheese topping:** In a separate bowl, combine the mozzarella, Romano, Parmesan, and bread crumbs. When well blended, stir in the garlic, olive oil, and parsley, and mix well.

3. **Make the ziti:** Preheat the oven to 375°F. Coat a 9 x 13-inch baking dish with cooking spray or a little olive oil.

4. Pour ½ cup of the ziti sauce in the dish and spread it evenly over the bottom.

5. Mix the cooked ziti with the remaining ziti sauce, stirring to coat it well. Pour the pasta into the dish and spread it evenly over the bottom. Sprinkle with the shredded mozzarella.

6. Spread the cheese topping evenly over everything. Bake for about 30 minutes, or until the top is golden brown and the cheese is bubbling.

7. Let the dish sit about 5 minutes before serving.

Makes 6 to 8 servings

Add roasted chicken, vegetables, or crumbled hamburger meat to this classic dish on leftover night!

OLIVE GARDEN
Baked Mostaccioli

A DECEPTIVELY SIMPLE CROWD-PLEASER. THE CHEESE, CREAM, AND BUTTER FOLDED
INTO SAVORY RAGU SAUCE WILL MAKE YOUR FAMILY GO BACK FOR SECONDS.

1½ sticks (6 ounces) unsalted
butter

1 cup heavy (whipping) cream

1 teaspoon kosher salt

¼ teaspoon white pepper

1½ cups grated Parmesan cheese

1 pound mostaccioli pasta,
cooked according to package
directions

¼ cup chopped fresh flat-leaf
parsley

2 large cloves garlic, minced

1 (26-ounce) jar spaghetti sauce

3 (5-ounce) boneless, skinless
chicken breasts, cooked and
chopped

½ cup shredded mozzarella
cheese

1. Preheat the oven to 350°F.

2. In a large skillet, melt the butter over medium heat. Whisk in the heavy
   cream, salt, and white pepper. When the sauce is thickened, add the Parmesan and stir until melted. Add the cooked mostaccioli and stir until it
   is well coated.

3. Stir in the parsley, garlic, and spaghetti sauce. Add the cooked chicken
   and simmer over low heat for about 5 minutes.

4. Pour the mixture into a 9 x 13-inch baking dish and top with the mozzarella. Bake for 25 to 30 minutes, or until the top is lightly browned and
   the cheese is bubbling.

Makes 6 to 8 servings

*No mostaccioli in the pantry? Use penne, rigatoni, or fusilli
pasta instead.*

PANDA EXPRESS
Cream Cheese Rangoons

RANGOONS ARE AN OLD FAVORITE FROM THE TIKI CUISINE HEYDAY OF DON THE BEACHCOMBER, WHO IS KNOWN AS THE FOUNDING FATHER OF TIKI RESTAURANTS. THESE APPETIZERS ARE SURPRISINGLY STILL POPULAR AND KEEP POPPING UP IN VARIOUS ITERATIONS AT RESTAURANTS THROUGHOUT THE COUNTRY. THE KIDS WILL LOVE THE CRISPY FRIED WONTONS WITH AN OLD-TIME SWEET AND SOUR SAUCE.

Sweet and Sour Sauce
¾ cup pineapple juice

½ cup distilled white vinegar

½ cup sugar

2 tablespoons cocktail sauce

¼ teaspoon ground ginger

½ teaspoon granulated garlic

¼ teaspoon red pepper flakes

2 tablespoons cornstarch

¼ cup cold water

Rangoons
1 (8-ounce) package cream cheese, softened

2 green onions, thinly sliced

½ teaspoon granulated garlic

12 wonton wrappers

2 cups canola oil, for deep-frying

1. **Make the sweet and sour sauce:** In a small saucepan, stir together the pineapple juice, vinegar, and sugar over medium heat until the sugar dissolves.

2. Whisk in the cocktail sauce, ginger, garlic, and pepper flakes. Bring the sauce to a boil, then reduce the heat and let it simmer for 5 minutes.

3. In a small bowl, make a paste of the cornstarch and cold water. Whisk it into the simmering sauce and stir until the sauce thickens. Take it off the heat and set it aside.

4. **Make the rangoons:** In a bowl, stir together the cream cheese, green onions, and garlic.

5. Place a rounded spoonful of the mixture into the center of each wonton wrapper. Run a wet finger around the edges of the wonton, pull the sides up, and squeeze them together to form a packet.

6. In a heavy-bottomed saucepan or electric fryer, heat the oil to 375°F (use a deep-fry thermometer).

7. Drop the rangoons in the hot oil, a few at a time, until they are crispy and browned on all sides. Remove them with a slotted spoon and let them drain on paper towels until they are all fried.

8. Serve the rangoons on a platter surrounding a bowl of the sauce.

Makes 4 servings

Add diced red bell pepper, chopped water chestnuts, or chopped snow peas to the cream cheese mixture for more flavor and texture. It only takes a small amount of any ingredient, chopped finely, to make your own signature rangoon!

PANERA BREAD
Broccoli Cheddar Soup

PANERA'S VERSION OF CREAM OF BROCCOLI SOUP USES HALF-AND-HALF TO LIGHTEN UP THE PUREE AND SOME GOOD, SHARP CHEDDAR TO GIVE IT SOME DEPTH. THIS IS AN EASY SOUP TO PREPARE AT HOME AND WORKS AS AN AFTER-SCHOOL SNACK AS WELL AS A STARTER FOR DINNER.

2 cups broccoli florets	½ teaspoon kosher salt
1 tablespoon olive oil	¼ teaspoon pepper
1 yellow onion, chopped	Scant ¼ teaspoon ground
1 rib celery, chopped	nutmeg
1 cup chicken broth	1½ cups shredded Cheddar
1½ cups half-and-half	cheese
1 teaspoon dried thyme	1 carrot, peeled and shredded

1. Microwave the broccoli florets for 4 minutes. Reserve 6 small florets for garnish.

2. In a large saucepan, heat the oil over medium heat. Add the onion and celery and cook until soft.

3. Add the chicken broth, half-and-half, thyme, salt, pepper, and nutmeg. Bring to a boil, then reduce the heat and add all the broccoli except for the garnish. Simmer until all the vegetables are cooked through.

4. Puree the soup in a blender, working in batches if necessary, and return the puree to the saucepan over low heat.

5. Stir in the Cheddar and carrot, and stir until the cheese melts. Adjust the seasonings with salt and pepper, if desired.

6. Serve the soup garnished with the broccoli florets.

Makes 6 servings

If you're out of Cheddar, provolone, Gruyère, or Gouda all make great melting cheeses.

PANERA BREAD
Chewy Chocolate Chip Cookies

THESE ARE A BIG HIT AT PANERA BREAD. THE DOUGH IS FROZEN BEFORE BAKING, MAKING THEM IDEAL FOR A QUICK TREAT FOR UNEXPECTED GUESTS OR TO JUST KEEP ON HAND.

4¼ cups all-purpose flour
2 tablespoons cornstarch
2 teaspoons baking soda
1 teaspoon kosher salt
2 sticks (½ pound) unsalted butter, softened
½ cup vegetable shortening

1½ cups packed golden brown sugar
2 eggs
1 tablespoon vanilla extract
12 ounces semisweet chocolate chips

1. In a bowl, whisk together the flour, cornstarch, baking soda, and salt.

2. In a separate bowl, with an electric mixer, cream the butter and shortening. When smooth and well blended, add the brown sugar and beat until light and fluffy. Add the eggs, one at a time, beating after each addition. Add the vanilla. Stir in the chocolate chips.

3. Stir the flour mixture into the butter and sugar mixture and mix until blended.

4. Use an ice cream scoop or melon baller and form the dough into 24 balls. Place the balls on a parchment-lined baking sheet and freeze until needed.

5. Preheat the oven to 350°F. Line a baking sheet with parchment paper.

6. Place the frozen cookies at least 2 inches apart on the baking sheet. Bake for about 15 minutes or until the edges are lightly browned, then let cool on a wire rack.

Makes 2 dozen cookies

When the cookies are frozen solid, they can be sealed in a plastic bag and kept in the freezer for up to 3 months. Take out as many as you want to bake at a time and keep the remainder frozen.

PANERA BREAD
Peanut Butter & Jelly Sandwich

YOU CAN USE ANY OF YOUR FAVORITE PANERA BREADS TO MAKE THESE SANDWICHES, BUT THEY ARE PROBABLY BEST WITH THE ALL NATURAL WHITE BREAD.

2 tablespoons unsalted butter, softened

8 slices white bread

½ cup peanut butter, creamy or chunky

½ cup Concord grape jelly or strawberry jam

1. Heat a griddle or large skillet over medium heat.

2. Butter one side of each of the slices of bread.

3. On the unbuttered sides, spread 4 of the slices with the peanut butter and 4 of the slices with the jelly or jam. Close up the sandwiches buttered side out.

4. Grill them, buttered side down on the hot griddle. Flip when toasted on one side to toast on the other.

5. Slice each sandwich diagonally and serve hot.

Makes 4 sandwiches

Sometimes this is all a youngster needs for lunch. Add a glass of milk and a few carrot sticks and it will hold them until dinner.

PANERA BREAD
Low-Fat Mango Smoothie

TRY TO USE FRESH FRUITS AND JUICES TO MAKE THIS SMOOTHIE. IF FRESH MAN-
GOES AND ORANGE JUICE ARE OUT OF SEASON, USE THE LEAST PROCESSED BRAND
YOU CAN FIND.

3 mangoes, peeled and chopped,
   or 4 cups thawed frozen
1½ cups fresh orange juice
2 ripe medium bananas, sliced
1 cup Greek nonfat vanilla yogurt

1 cup ice cubes
¼ cup honey or maple syrup
Pinch of ground nutmeg
Mint sprigs, for garnish (optional)

1. In a blender, combine the mangoes, orange juice, and bananas and process until smooth.
2. Add the vanilla yogurt, ice cubes, honey, and nutmeg and process on
   high speed until smooth.
3. Divide among 6 chilled glasses and garnish with mint leaves, if desired.

Makes 6 servings

*Greek yogurt will hold up best to this amount of high speed
processing. For a milkshake-like consistency, stir it in after the
rest of the ingredients have been blended.*

PANERA BREAD
Mac and Cheese

PANERA BREAD'S MAC AND CHEESE IS REALLY SIMPLE TO MAKE AT HOME. THEIR SECRET IS A SMIDGE OF DIJON MUSTARD WHICH BALANCES NICELY WITH THE CREAMINESS OF THE PASTA AND MILK.

2 cups elbow macaroni or pasta shells, cooked according to package directions
2½ cups milk
½ teaspoon kosher salt

1 teaspoon Dijon mustard
1 tablespoon unsalted butter
1 cup grated sharp white Cheddar cheese

1. Rinse the pasta under hot water.
2. In a medium saucepan, combine the milk, salt, mustard, and butter. Bring the mixture to a simmer over medium-high heat and stir in the pasta shells. Simmer the mixture for 5 minutes, stirring frequently, until the pasta has absorbed the milk.
3. Remove the pan from the heat and stir in the Cheddar. Cover for a few minutes to let the cheese melt, then serve hot.

Makes 3 or 4 servings

PANERA BREAD
Strawberries and Cream Scones

YOU DON'T NEED TO ADD THE TOPPING TO ENJOY THESE DELICATE SCONES, BUT THE LITTLE BIT OF ICING DRIZZLED OVER ADDS THE PERFECT AMOUNT OF SWEETNESS.

Scones

1 ¼ cups diced strawberries
¼ cup half-and-half
2 cups all-purpose flour
¼ cup sugar
1 tablespoon baking powder

½ teaspoon fine sea salt
6 tablespoons (¾ stick) unsalted cold butter, cut in pieces
1 egg
2 teaspoons vanilla extract

Topping

3 tablespoons sugar
2 teaspoons milk

1 ½ teaspoons vanilla extract

1. **Make the scones:** Preheat the oven to 375°F. Line 2 baking sheets with parchment paper (or lightly coat them with vegetable shortening or cooking spray).

2. In a blender, combine ½ cup of the strawberries and the half-and-half and process until smooth. Set aside.

3. In a bowl, whisk together the flour, sugar, baking powder, and salt. Use a pastry blender or your fingers to cut in the butter, working it until it is the texture of coarse grain.

4. In a separate bowl, whisk together the pureed strawberry mixture, egg, and vanilla. Stir this mixture into the dry ingredients, and add the remaining diced strawberries and stir until well blended.

5. Drop the dough by heaping spoonfuls onto the prepared baking sheets. Each scone should be about the size of a golf ball.

6. Bake the scones for 14 to 15 minutes, or until they just begin to brown around the edges.

7. **Meanwhile, make the topping:** In a small microwave-safe bowl, combine the sugar and milk. Microwave on high for 20 to 30 seconds, or until the mixture is bubbling.

8. Stir in the vanilla extract and mix until the topping is well blended.

9. Using a small spoon, drizzle the topping in a zigzag motion over the tops of the hot scones. Let the scones sit for a few minutes before serving to let the topping set up.

Makes 10 servings

You can also use a scone pan with this recipe, although you will need to increase the baking time to 18 to 20 minutes.

PEPPERIDGE FARM

Orange Milano Cookies

PEPPERIDGE FARM COOKIES HAVE BEEN FAVORITES FOR YEARS AND SOME HAVE ACHIEVED CLASSIC STATUS. ALTHOUGH SOLD AT ALMOST ALL MAJOR GROCERY STORES, THE HOME-BAKED VERSION OF THIS ORANGE MILANO COOKIE CAN'T BE BEAT.

Butter or cooking spray, for the pan
3¼ cups all-purpose flour
2 teaspoons cornstarch
1 teaspoon fine sea salt
1 teaspoon baking powder
½ teaspoon baking soda
2 sticks (½ pound) unsalted butter, softened

1 cup granulated sugar
1 cup packed golden brown sugar
2 eggs
1 teaspoon vanilla extract
1 teaspoon orange extract
1 tablespoon grated orange zest
8 ounces milk chocolate chips
8 ounces semisweet chocolate chips

1. Preheat the oven to 350°F. Butter a baking sheet or line it with parchment paper and coat the paper with cooking spray.

2. In a bowl, whisk together the flour, cornstarch, salt, baking powder, and baking soda.

3. In a separate bowl, with an electric mixer, cream the butter and both sugars until light and fluffy. Beat in the eggs, one at a time, and beat well after each addition.

4. Stir in the vanilla and orange extracts, orange zest, and both chocolate chips. Stir to thoroughly blend all the ingredients.

5. Drop by spoonfuls onto the baking sheet 2 inches apart and bake for 9 to 10 minutes until edges are firm. Let the cookies cool on the baking sheet, then transfer them to a wire rack to cool completely.

Makes about 4 dozen cookies

The two different types of chocolate give these cookies a nice contrast, but you can use all of one type if you desire.

P.F. CHANG'S
Chicken Fried Rice

CHICKEN FRIED RICE HAS EARNED ITS PLACE IN THE CHINESE-AMERICAN COM-
FORT FOOD HALL OF FAME. P.F. CHANG'S SERVES A LIGHTLY SEASONED VERSION
THAT IS PERFECT FOR GIVING KIDS THEIR FIRST TASTE OF ASIAN INGREDIENTS.

1 egg
½ teaspoon toasted sesame oil
1 (4-ounce) boneless, skinless
  chicken breast
Kosher salt and pepper
2 tablespoons peanut or canola
  oil
1 clove garlic, minced

½ teaspoon minced peeled fresh
  ginger
½ cup mixed vegetables, your
  own or thawed frozen
2 cups cooked white rice
  (long-grain, jasmine, or basmati)
2 tablespoons soy sauce
2 green onions, thinly sliced

1. In a small bowl, beat the egg. Whisk in the sesame oil and set it aside.

2. Season the chicken with salt and pepper and cut into bite-size pieces.

3. In a skillet or wok, heat 1 tablespoon of the oil over medium-high heat.
    Add the chicken and stir-fry until cooked through and no longer pink in
    the center. Remove it with a slotted spoon and keep it warm.

4. Add the remaining 1 tablespoon oil to the pan. Add the garlic and ginger
    and stir-fry until tender. Add the mixed vegetables and stir-fry until
    cooked through but still slightly firm.

5. Push the vegetables to the side of the wok or skillet and stir in the egg.
    Scramble the egg quickly, then add the chicken and cooked rice. Stir-fry
    all the ingredients until warmed through and well mixed.

6. Add the soy sauce and green onions and toss with the rice and vegeta-
    bles. Serve hot.

Makes 2 or 3 servings

*The mixed vegetables can be Asian inspired or very plain. Good
choices would be snow peas, water chestnuts, and bamboo
shoots, all cut fairly small. Green peas with small diced carrots
and red bell pepper would add color and texture to the stir-fry.*

P.F. CHANG'S
Crispy Honey Chicken

SWEET AND SAVORY, HOT AND CRUNCHY—JUST WHAT KIDS LOVE. SERVE THE DIPPING SAUCE IN THE CENTER OF A PLATTER WITH THE CHICKEN ALL AROUND FOR A PARTY DISH, OR SERVE THE SAUCE AND CHICKEN ON INDIVIDUAL PLATES FOR LUNCH OR DINNER. THE BATTER SHOULD BE MADE FIRST SO IT HAS TIME TO REST.

Batter

½ cup all-purpose flour
¼ cup cornstarch
¼ teaspoon baking powder
¼ teaspoon baking soda
1 egg, well beaten
⅔ cup ice water

Chicken and Marinade

1 tablespoon soy sauce
½ cup dry sherry, mirin, or sake
2 large cloves garlic, minced
¼ teaspoon white pepper
½ teaspoon kosher salt
2 tablespoons cornstarch
1 pound chicken tenders, cut into bite-size pieces

Honey Dipping Sauce

½ cup pineapple juice
½ cup honey
¼ cup apple cider vinegar
¼ cup soy sauce
2 tablespoons dark brown sugar
1 teaspoon minced peeled fresh ginger
¼ cup cornstarch
¼ cup cold water

Frying

2 to 3 cups canola oil, for deep-frying
2 green onions, thinly sliced

1. **Make the batter:** In a bowl, whisk together the flour, cornstarch, baking powder, and baking soda. Stir in the egg to make a paste, then whisk in the ice water until smooth. Cover and let it sit in the refrigerator for at least 30 minutes.

2. **Marinate the chicken:** In a large bowl, whisk together the soy sauce, dry sherry, and garlic.

3. Mix the white pepper, salt, and cornstarch and toss in a resealable plastic bag with the chicken pieces. Add the chicken to the soy sauce mixture and toss to coat the pieces evenly. Cover and marinate for at least 30 minutes.

4. **Make the honey dipping sauce:** In small saucepan, whisk together the pineapple juice, honey, vinegar, soy sauce, brown sugar, and ginger. Bring the mixture to a low boil, stirring to dissolve the sugar.

5. In a small bowl, make a paste of the cornstarch and water.

6. Whisk the paste into the sauce and let it simmer a few minutes until thickened.

7. **Fry the chicken:** Fill a heavy-bottomed saucepan or electric fryer halfway with the canola oil and heat to 375°F (use a deep-fry thermometer).

8. Take the chicken out of the marinade and shake off any excess. Working in batches, coat the chicken in the batter and fry in the hot oil until it's golden on all sides and cooked through. Drain on paper towels and keep warm while frying the rest of the chicken.

9. Scatter the green onion over the chicken and serve with the dipping sauce.

Makes 4 servings

Mirin is a sweet cooking wine made from rice that adds flavor and depth. It is very low in alcohol, which evaporates when heated.

RED LOBSTER
Broiled Dill Salmon

A QUICK AND EASY WAY TO GET HEALTHY FOOD IN LITTLE TUMMIES. CUT THE LARGE FILLETS IN HALF FOR A KID-SIZE MEAL, AND SERVE WITH A SALAD OR FRESH VEGETABLES.

8 tablespoons (1 stick) unsalted butter, melted
1 tablespoon fresh lemon juice
1 teaspoon kosher salt
¼ teaspoon pepper

1 tablespoon chopped fresh dill
¼ teaspoon red pepper flakes (optional)
4 (8-ounce) salmon fillets, about 1 inch thick (skin off)

1. Position a rack about 5 inches from the heat and preheat the broiler. Line a broiler pan with foil.

2. In a bowl, combine the melted butter, lemon juice, salt, pepper, and dill and stir to dissolve the salt. Add the pepper flakes (if using).

3. Brush the salmon with some of the butter mixture and arrange the fillets on the foil.

4. Broil for 5 to 8 minutes, or until just lightly charred on top. Remove the fillets, still on the foil, to a rimmed baking sheet or baking dish. Leave the oven on and turn from broil to bake and set the temperature at 400°F.

5. Brush the salmon with more of the butter mixture, return to the oven, and bake another 5 minutes, or just until the salmon is cooked through and flakes easily with a fork.

6. Serve with the remaining butter and dill sauce on the side.

Makes 4 servings

If you don't want to use your broiler or don't have one, simply bake the fillets at 400°F for about 10 minutes, basting often with the dill butter, until cooked through.

RED LOBSTER
Cheesecake

A SLIGHT TWIST TO THE CRUST OF THIS CREAMY DESSERT MAY MAKE IT ONE OF YOUR FAVORITE GO-TO RECIPES. A CRUSHED PACKAGE OF LORNA DOONE COOKIES TAKES THE PLACE OF GRAHAM CRACKERS FOR A RICHER SHORTBREAD CRUST.

Crust

Cooking spray or shortening, for the pan

1 (10-ounce) package Lorna Doone or other shortbread cookies, crushed, plus extra for garnish

8 tablespoons (1 stick) unsalted butter, melted

¼ cup sugar

1 envelope unflavored gelatin

Filling

1 pound cream cheese, softened

1 cup sour cream

2 eggs

2 tablespoons unsalted butter, softened

2 tablespoons cornstarch

1 cup sugar

1 teaspoon vanilla extract

1. **Make the crust:** Preheat the oven to 350°F. Lightly coat the sides of a 9-inch springform pan with cooking spray or shortening.

2. In a small bowl, combine the crushed cookies, melted butter, sugar, and gelatin.

3. Pat the crust in an even layer across the bottom and up the inside of the springform pan. Bake for 8 minutes. Set the crust aside. (Leave the oven on.)

4. **Make the filling:** In a medium bowl, with an electric mixer, combine the cream cheese, sour cream, eggs, butter, cornstarch, sugar, and vanilla and beat until the mixture is smooth and creamy.

5. Pour the mixture into the baked crust and bake for 35 to 40 minutes, or until a knife inserted into the center comes out clean.

6. Let the cheesecake cool for about an hour and then refrigerate for at least 4 hours before serving.

7. Sprinkle with the reserved cookie crumbs and serve.

Makes 8 servings

A pan of hot water on the rack below the cake will keep the surface from cracking. You can also bake the cake in a water bath; tightly seal the springform pan with foil beforehand.

RED LOBSTER
Garlic-Grilled Shrimp

A DELICIOUS, CLASSIC DISH KIDS WILL DEVOUR AT THE DINNER TABLE.

8 tablespoons (1 stick) unsalted
   butter
2 cloves garlic, minced
¼ teaspoon Worcestershire
   sauce

¼ cup lemon juice
Kosher salt and pepper
2 pounds medium shrimp, peeled
   and deveined

1. In a large saucepan, melt the butter over medium heat. Add the garlic and cook until softened.

2. Remove the pan from the heat and stir in the Worcestershire sauce, lemon juice, salt, and pepper. Let the mixture cool slightly (but not harden).

3. Toss the shrimp with the garlic butter and marinate for 30 minutes.

4. Thread the shrimp on metal or bamboo skewers (soaked 30 minutes before using) and grill or broil until cooked through.

5. Serve hot.

Makes 8 servings

The cooked shrimp can also be refrigerated and served cold with a spicy mayonnaise dip, or used in a salad of mixed greens and grilled vegetables.

RED ROBIN
Strawberry Lemonade

NOTHING IS AS REFRESHING ON A HOT SUMMER DAY AS ICE-COLD LEMONADE.
THE KIDS WILL LOVE THIS STRAWBERRY VERSION.

Lemon Syrup
1½ cups sugar
1½ cups water

Zest of 1 lemon, cut into thin
strips

Strawberry Syrup
1 pint strawberries, hulled and
chopped

½ cup sugar

Lemonade
2 cups fresh lemon juice, pulp
strained

¼ teaspoon kosher salt
2 cups cold water

1. **Make the lemon syrup:** In a medium saucepan, combine the sugar, water, and lemon zest. Bring the mixture to a boil, stirring to dissolve the sugar.

2. When the sugar is dissolved, remove the pan from the heat and let it cool to room temperature. Remove the strips of lemon zest.

3. **Make the strawberry syrup:** Combine the strawberries and sugar in a small bowl. Stir the mixture with a wooden spoon, then set it aside for 45 minutes to let the sugar dissolve in the strawberry juice.

4. Strain the mixture, reserving the berries and juice separately.

5. **Make the lemonade:** In a large pitcher, combine the lemon syrup, lemon juice, salt, and cold water.

6. Fill a tall glass with ice and add a tablespoon of the strawberry syrup. Fill the glass with the lemonade, stir, and add a few of the reserved strawberries.

Makes 8 to 10 servings

*Try raspberry or blackberry lemonade with fresh berries, or
stone fruit such as peaches and apricots.*

RUBY TUESDAY
Chicken Quesadillas

WHEN THE KIDS NEED JUST A LITTLE SOMETHING TO HOLD THEM OVER UNTIL DINNER, THIS QUICKLY ASSEMBLED QUESADILLA FITS THE BILL. USE LEFTOVER CHICKEN AND A JAR OF SALSA IF YOU DON'T HAVE TIME FOR ALL THE SLICING AND DICING.

4 ounces cooked chicken breast, shredded or diced
1 tablespoon Italian dressing
1 tablespoon unsalted butter
1 (12-inch) flour tortilla
1 cup shredded Monterey Jack cheese
1 small tomato, diced
1 teaspoon Southwestern seasoning
2 tablespoons sour cream
½ cup fresh salsa, for dipping

1. In a bowl, toss the cooked chicken with the Italian dressing and let it marinate for about 30 minutes.

2. When ready to serve, in a skillet, melt the butter over medium-low heat. Lay the tortilla on top. Fill one side of the tortilla with the chicken. Scatter the cheese over the chicken. Sprinkle with the tomato and Southwestern seasoning. Dot with the sour cream.

3. Fold the unfilled side of the tortilla over the filled half and cook until the cheese starts to melt. Flip the quesadilla over to toast the other side.

4. Remove the quesadilla from the skillet and cut into 6 wedges. Serve with salsa for dipping.

Makes 6 portions

Fill your quesadilla with whatever you have in the refrigerator—vegetables, rice, beans, or meat are all excellent fillings. Just be sure to melt shredded cheese over all the ingredients.

SONIC

Cherry Limeade

KEEP CANS OF LIMEADE IN THE FREEZER TO WHIP UP THIS FIZZY BEVERAGE WHEN-
EVER THE KIDS NEED A TREAT.

1 (12-ounce) can frozen limeade
concentrate
1 (2-liter) bottle lemon-lime soda

¼ cup grenadine
1 lime, cut into thin wedges

1. In a large bowl, dissolve the frozen limeade in the lemon-lime soda. Stir in the grenadine.
2. Pour the mixture into tall glasses filled with ice and garnish with a lime wedge.

Makes 6 to 8 servings

*If you don't have grenadine on hand, you can always drain a
jar of maraschino cherries and use the juice. Then garnish your
limeade with a cherry!*

STARBUCKS
Passion Tea Lemonade

THIS TEA IS JUST AS TASTY AS THE ORIGINAL FROM STARBUCKS. KEEP A PITCHER OF IT IN THE REFRIGERATOR FOR WHEN YOU NEED A LIFT.

2 bags Tazo Passion herbal tea
2 cups boiling water
2 teaspoons sugar

¼ teaspoon vanilla extract
½ cup lemonade

1. Place the tea bags in a heatproof container. Pour the boiling water over the tea bags. Add the sugar and vanilla. Let the tea steep for 15 minutes.

2. Remove the bags and refrigerate for at least 1 hour before serving.

3. Stir in the lemonade and serve in a glass of ice.

Makes 2 to 4 servings

Tazo tea is available from markets, online retailers, and Starbucks. Their Passion tea is a blend of hibiscus, orange peel, rose hips, and passion fruit.

STARBUCKS
Petite Vanilla Scones

STARBUCKS SELLS THESE SCONES BECAUSE THEY KNOW YOU'LL NEED COFFEE TO
GO WITH THEM. THE KIDS WILL LOVE THEM WITH A CUP OF HOT COCOA.

2 cups all-purpose flour
½ cup sugar
2 teaspoons baking powder
½ teaspoon baking soda
½ teaspoon fine sea salt

5 tablespoons unsalted butter,
    diced
1 cup sour cream
1 egg yolk
2 teaspoons vanilla extract

Sugar Glaze
¼ cup hot milk, plus more if
    needed

1 cup powdered sugar

1. Preheat the oven to 400°F. Line a baking sheet with parchment paper.

2. In a bowl, whisk together the flour, sugar, baking powder, baking soda,
    and salt. Cut the pieces of butter in with a pastry blender or use your
    fingers so that the mixture resembles coarse grain.

3. In a separate bowl, beat together the sour cream, egg yolk, and vanilla
    until creamy.

4. Fold the sour cream mixture into the dry ingredients and stir together
    with a fork until the dough forms a ball. Make sure you scrape up all the
    pieces of dough clinging to the bowl.

5. Place the dough on the baking sheet and pat it into a disk about 1 inch
    high. Cut the dough into wedges but do not separate them. Bake for 15
    minutes or until golden brown on top.

6. **Meanwhile, make the glaze:** In a small bowl, slowly pour the hot milk into the powdered sugar, whisking constantly. Add a little more milk, a spoonful at a time if the glaze is too stiff.

7. Brush the warm scones with the glaze.

Makes 8 scones

You might also want to bake these in a scone pan if you have one available. These are round or square pans with divided sections that the dough is pressed into. The yield will vary depending on the pan used.

STARBUCKS
Salted Caramel Sweet Squares

THESE ADDICTIVE MORSELS HAVE JUST THE PERFECT BALANCE OF SWEET AND SALTY. IT MIGHT NOT BE A BAD IDEA TO INDIVIDUALLY WRAP EACH SQUARE AND KEEP THEM IN A CUPBOARD AWAY FROM PRYING LITTLE FINGERS!

Caramel Pretzel Crust

Cooking spray
⅓ cup packed golden brown sugar
4 tablespoons (½ stick) unsalted butter, softened
2 teaspoons vanilla extract

¼ teaspoon fine sea salt
¾ cup all-purpose flour
80 small soft caramel candies
¼ cup milk
1½ cups pecans, finely chopped
2 cups crushed pretzels

Chocolate Fudge

1½ cups sugar
½ cup evaporated milk
2 tablespoons unsalted butter

2 cups mini marshmallows
2 cups semisweet chocolate chips
1 teaspoon vanilla extract

1. **Make the caramel pretzel crust:** Preheat the oven to 375°F. Coat a 9 x 13-inch baking pan with cooking spray.

2. In a bowl, with an electric mixer, beat the brown sugar and butter until light and fluffy. Beat in 1 teaspoon of the vanilla and the sea salt.

3. Add the flour to the beaten ingredients and stir until well blended.

4. Firmly press the mixture into the bottom of the baking pan and bake for 15 minutes.

5. Meanwhile, in a small saucepan, combine the caramel candies and milk and cook over low heat until the candy melts, stirring frequently. Stir in the remaining 1 teaspoon vanilla, then remove the pan from the heat. Measure out a few spoonfuls and set aside for swirling over the top of the fudge layer.

6. In a bowl, mix the pecans and pretzels.

7. When the crust is ready, remove it from the oven and pour the caramel mixture over the hot crust. Sprinkle the pecan-pretzel mixture over the caramel.

8. Return the pan to the oven and bake for 15 minutes. Let it cool completely on a wire rack.

9. **Make the chocolate fudge:** In a medium saucepan, combine the sugar, evaporated milk, and butter. Bring the mixture to a rolling boil, stirring constantly. Boil for 4 minutes.

10. Remove the pan from the heat and stir in the marshmallows and chocolate chips. Stir until both items have melted. Stir in the vanilla.

11. Pour the fudge mixture over the top of the cooled crust mixture. Warm the reserved spoonfuls of caramel mixture with a pinch of salt and drizzle it over the top of the fudge. Use a knife to gently run through the salted caramel drizzles to make sure it is swirled throughout the fudge.

12. Chill the fudge crust until firm, then cut into squares.

Makes 15 to 20 squares

If tightly wrapped, these squares can be frozen for up to a month. Be sure to let them thaw out in the refrigerator before unwrapping.

STARBUCK'S
Vanilla Bean Cupcakes

THESE CUPCAKES WILL FILL YOUR KITCHEN WITH THE MOST DELICIOUS SCENT OF
VANILLA. YOU'LL NEVER WANT TO LEAVE THE HOUSE!

Cupcakes

1¾ cups cake flour
1½ teaspoons baking powder
½ teaspoon baking soda
½ teaspoon fine sea salt
4 tablespoons (½ stick) unsalted
  butter, softened
1 cup sugar

2 eggs
1 teaspoon vanilla extract
1 vanilla bean, split lengthwise
⅓ cup sour cream
¼ cup canola oil
⅔ cup milk

Vanilla Buttercream

8 tablespoons (1 stick) unsalted
  butter, softened
½ vanilla bean
½ teaspoon vanilla extract

Pinch of sea salt
¼ cup milk
3½ cups powdered sugar, plus
  more if needed

1. **Make the cupcakes:** Preheat the oven to 350°F. Line 12 muffin cups
    with paper liners.

2. In a bowl, whisk together the flour, baking powder, baking soda, and
    salt.

3. In a separate bowl, with an electric mixer, beat the butter and sugar
    until creamy. Beat in the eggs, one at time, beating after each addition.
    Stir in the vanilla extract. Scrape the vanilla seeds into the dough and
    mix on high speed a few seconds to disperse the seeds throughout the
    mixture. Beat in the sour cream until just blended, then stir in the oil
    and mix well.

4. Add the butter and sugar mixture to the flour mixture and stir just until
    mixed. With the mixer on low speed, slowly beat the milk into the batter.

5. Fill the muffin cups halfway with the batter and bake for 18 to 20 minutes, or until a toothpick inserted into the center comes out clean. If the cupcakes are not done, bake 2 to 4 minutes longer. Let the cupcakes cool on a wire rack before frosting.

6. **Make the frosting:** In a bowl, with an electric mixer, cream the butter until smooth. Scrape in the vanilla seeds and mix at high speed a few seconds to disperse the seeds throughout the butter. Beat in the vanilla extract, salt, and milk and mix until well combined.

7. Sift the powdered sugar over the butter mixture and stir until the frosting is very smooth. Add a little extra sugar if necessary to get it to a good frosting consistency.

8. Use a small spoon or metal spatula to frost the top of each cupcake.

Makes 12 cupcakes

These cupcakes are very moist and will not turn golden brown in the oven, so testing for doneness is the best way to see if they have baked long enough.

STEAK 'N SHAKE
Frisco Melt

STEAK 'N SHAKE HAS BEEN AROUND FOR 80 YEARS, AND THERE ARE MANY THINGS THEY DO JUST RIGHT, INCLUDING THIS DOUBLE-BEEF, TWO-CHEESE SANDWICH. IT'S A FILLING MEAL IN ITSELF, BUT YOU CAN ADD FRIES AND A SOFT DRINK FOR A REAL RESTAURANT EXPERIENCE.

Frisco Sauce

¼ cup Thousand Island dressing, store-bought or homemade

2 tablespoons French dressing

Sandwiches

1 pound lean ground chuck or sirloin

Kosher salt and pepper

2 tablespoons unsalted butter, softened

8 slices sourdough bread

4 slices Swiss cheese

4 slices American cheese

1. **Make the Frisco sauce:** Whisk together the Thousand Island and French dressings and set aside.

2. **Make the sandwiches:** Divide the beef evenly into 8 portions and shape them into patties. Season them with salt and pepper and set aside.

3. Butter each slice of bread on one side. Heat a large skillet or griddle over medium-low heat and toast the bread, butter side down, until golden brown. Set the toast aside.

4. Increase the heat to medium-high under the skillet and cook the patties, turning once, until cooked to your desired doneness.

5. To assemble a sandwich, put a piece of the sourdough toasted side down on a work surface. Top with a slice of Swiss cheese. Lay a cooked patty on the Swiss cheese and top with the American cheese. Follow with another patty. Spread the untoasted side of a slice of sourdough with the Frisco sauce and place it over the rest of the sandwich.

6. Make the rest of the sandwiches in the same manner. Slice them in half before serving for easier eating.

Makes 4 servings

You can get the cheese really melted if you set the sandwich back on the griddle before serving. Wipe out the skillet or griddle and grill the sandwich on one side for about a minute, then carefully flip it over and grill the other side.

SUBWAY
Meatball Marinara

SUBWAY HAS A HIT ON ITS HANDS WITH THIS MEATBALL SUB. THEY USE LEAN GROUND BEEF AND REDUCED-FAT CHEESE TO KEEP THE CALORIES DOWN. USE COOKING SPRAY TO SAUTÉ THE VEGETABLES, AND COOK THE MEATBALLS IN THE SAUCE TO AVOID HAVING TO SEAR THEM IN OIL.

Meatballs
10 ounces lean ground chuck or sirloin
¼ cup unseasoned dried bread crumbs
¼ cup egg substitute
2 teaspoons dried parsley
1 teaspoon granulated garlic
1 teaspoon dried minced onion
1 teaspoon kosher salt
½ teaspoon pepper

Marinara Sauce
Olive oil cooking spray
⅓ cup finely chopped yellow onion
2 cloves garlic, minced
1 (14.5-ounce) can crushed tomatoes
2 teaspoons sugar
2 teaspoons dried oregano
1 teaspoon extra virgin olive oil

Sandwiches
4 (6-inch) submarine sandwich rolls
4 slices reduced-fat cheese, such as Swiss, Cheddar, provolone, pepper Jack, or mozzarella

1. **Make the meatballs:** In a medium bowl, combine the ground beef, bread crumbs, egg substitute, parsley, garlic, onion, salt, and pepper. Mix the ingredients with your hands until well combined.

2. Roll the mixture into 16 meatballs of equal size. Set them on a tray and refrigerate until needed.

3. **Make the marinara:** Spray a medium saucepan with cooking spray and heat over medium heat. Add the onion and garlic and cook until soft and translucent. Stir in the crushed tomatoes, sugar, oregano, and olive oil.

4. Add the meatballs to the saucepan and bring to a boil. Reduce the heat and let the sauce simmer for about 15 minutes, or until the meatballs are cooked through and no longer pink in the center.

5. **Make the sandwiches:** Split the rolls and layer each one with 4 meatballs. Spoon a little sauce over them and top with a slice of cheese. Cut the sub in half diagonally.

Makes 4 servings

You can make the meatballs ahead of time and freeze them, tightly wrapped in plastic wrap. You can also make the marinara meatball sauce and freeze it in a tightly closed jar for up to a month, or keep it refrigerated for up to a week. In both cases, make sure the sauce has cooled down before covering and freezing to minimize condensation.

SUBWAY
White Chocolate Raspberry Cheesecake Cookies

THESE LITTLE INDIVIDUAL CHEESECAKE BITES ARE LOADED WITH WHITE CHOCO-
LATE AND RASPBERRIES. THE CREAM CHEESE AND BUTTER MAKE THEM MOIST AND
DENSE. THEY CAN LAST UP TO A WEEK IN A COVERED CONTAINER, BUT LET'S FACE
IT—THEY PROBABLY WON'T LAST THAT LONG!

1½ cups all-purpose flour

2 teaspoons cornstarch

1 teaspoon baking soda

¼ teaspoon fine sea salt

8 tablespoons (1 stick) unsalted butter, softened

4 ounces cream cheese, softened

¾ cup granulated sugar

½ cup packed light brown sugar

1 egg

1 teaspoon vanilla extract

1 cup white chocolate chips

1 cup dried raspberries

1. In bowl, whisk together the flour, cornstarch, baking soda, and salt.

2. In a separate bowl, with an electric mixer, cream the butter and cream cheese with both sugars until light and fluffy. Beat in the egg and vanilla.

3. Stir the butter mixture into the flour mixture. When well blended, stir in the white chocolate chips and raspberries.

4. Turn the dough out onto a large sheet of plastic wrap and cover tightly. Refrigerate the dough for at least 30 minutes.

5. Preheat the oven to 350°F. Line 2 baking sheets with parchment paper or a silicone baking mat.

6. Form the dough into balls of about 2 tablespoons each. Place the dough on the baking sheets and lightly flatten them with the back of a wooden spoon or the bottom of a water glass.

7. Bake for 12 to 13 minutes or until the edges are firm and bottoms are lightly browned, then let them cool on a wire rack.

* * * * * * * * * *

Makes about 2 dozen cookies

* * * * * * * * * *

You may be able to find freeze-dried raspberries to use instead of dried. Freeze-drying retains all the nutrients of fresh berries, and it also preserves the fruit without having to add sugar. Any leftover rasberries are great as snacks for lunch bags or sprinkled over cereal in the morning.

TGI FRIDAYS
Chicken and Cheese

TGI FRIDAYS SENDS THIS MEAL OUT ON A SIZZLING PLATTER. YOU PROBABLY DON'T NEED TO BE DEALING WITH SIZZLING PLATTERS WITH HUNGRY YOUNG ONES AROUND, SO USE A CAST-IRON STEAK PAN OR RIDGED GRIDDLE FOR THIS ONE-PAN MEAL. PACKAGED MASHED POTATOES SAVE LOTS OF TIME AND TASTE JUST LIKE THE CREAMY ONES ON THE TGI FRIDAYS MENU.

Chicken and Marinade

2 (6-ounce) boneless, skinless chicken breasts
¼ cup olive oil

3 large cloves garlic, minced
1 teaspoon kosher salt
½ teaspoon pepper

Pepper Mix

2 tablespoons olive oil
1 large red bell pepper, cut into strips
1 large green bell pepper, cut into strips

1 yellow onion, cut into strips
2 large cloves garlic, minced
1 teaspoon kosher salt
½ teaspoon pepper

Creamy Mashed Potatoes

1 (24-ounce) package Ore-Ida Steam n' Mash Cut Russet potatoes
⅔ cup milk

¼ cup sour cream
3 tablespoons unsalted butter
1 teaspoon kosher salt
½ teaspoon pepper

Finishing

½ cup Monterey Jack cheese
½ cup Cheddar cheese

2 tablespoons chopped fresh parsley

1. **Marinate the chicken:** Pound the chicken breasts between two sheets of plastic wrap until they are even thickness.
2. In a shallow container, whisk together the olive oil, garlic, salt, and pepper. Coat the chicken with the marinade and refrigerate for at least 3 hours.

3. **Make the pepper mix:** In a large skillet, heat the oil over medium heat. Add the bell peppers and onion and cook until softened, about 2 minutes. Add the garlic and sauté a few minutes more, then season with the salt and pepper. Transfer to a bowl to keep warm. Keep the skillet at hand.

4. **Make the creamy mashed potatoes:** Microwave the potatoes according to package directions.

5. Transfer the hot potatoes to a large bowl, add the milk, sour cream, and butter and use a potato masher or a large fork to mash until smooth. Season with the salt and pepper.

6. **Finish the dish:** Use the same skillet the peppers and onions were cooked in, wiped with a paper towel. Heat the skillet over medium-high heat. Remove the chicken from the marinade, add to the pan, and cook, turning once, until cooked through and no longer pink in the center.

7. Heat a large cast-iron skillet over medium-high heat until very hot, then remove it from the heat. Heap the mashed potatoes to one side of the skillet and sprinkle the Monterey Jack and Cheddar on the other half.

8. Arrange the pepper medley over the potatoes and cheeses, then place the chicken breasts on top. Sprinkle with the chopped parsley and serve hot.

Makes 2 to 4 servings

TGI Fridays uses American and Mexican cheeses for this dish. Look for Chihuahua or Oaxaca cheeses in your market's refrigerator case—they are both light cow's milk cheeses that melt easily.

TGI FRIDAYS
Oreo Madness

PERFECT DESSERT FOR CHOCOLATE LOVERS.

8 tablespoons (1 stick) unsalted
butter, melted
1 (18-ounce) package Oreo
cookies, crushed
Cooking spray

1 quart strawberry ice cream,
slightly softened
1 (16-ounce) bottle Ghirardelli
chocolate sauce

1. In a bowl, combine the melted butter and crushed Oreo cookies.
2. Coat the wells of an 18-cup muffin tin (see note) with cooking spray or use paper liners.
3. Press a tablespoon of the cookie mixture into the bottom of each well. Pack each well about three-fourths of the way with the ice cream, then press on another tablespoon or so of the crumbled cookie mix.
4. Press down on the top layer and fill in with more crumbs. Make sure the ice cream is firmly packed in.
5. Cover the tin with plastic wrap and freeze for at least 2 hours.
6. When ready to serve, invert the muffin pan onto a work surface and tap the bottoms of the wells to free the ice cream sandwiches.
7. Drizzle with the chocolate sauce before serving.

Makes 18 servings

*You may need to use two 12-cup muffin tins if you don't have
(or can't find) a commercial 18-cup size.*

UNO PIZZERIA & GRILL
Deep-Dish Cookie Sundae

ANOTHER GUILTY PLEASURE THAT'S EASY TO MAKE USING PREMADE COOKIE DOUGH, ICE CREAM, AND CHOCOLATE SAUCE. YOU WILL NEED A 7-INCH CAKE PAN OR A DEEP-DISH PIZZA PAN TO MAKE IT JUST LIKE UNO'S.

Cooking spray
½ (16.5-ounce) roll refrigerated chocolate chip cookie dough or homemade dough

1 cup vanilla ice cream
½ cup whipped cream
¼ cup chocolate sauce, store-bought or homemade

1. Preheat the oven to the temperature listed on the cookie dough wrapper. Thoroughly coat a 7-inch cake pan with cooking spray.

2. Press the cookie dough evenly across the bottom of the pan and bake until done, according to the package directions.

3. Put the ice cream in the center of the cookie "pizza," pipe the whipped cream around it, drizzle a zigzag of chocolate sauce over the whole assembly, and serve warm.

Makes 2 to 4 servings

Put a cloth napkin or tea towel down on the table before serving the sundae; the pan may still be quite hot.

UNO PIZZERIA & GRILL
Pepperoni Deep-Dish Pizza

Pizza Dough

1 envelope active dry yeast
(2¼ teaspoons)
¾ cup hot water (110°F)
1 teaspoon sugar

¼ cup olive oil
2½ cups all-purpose flour
2 teaspoons kosher salt
1 tablespoon olive oil

Pepperoni Pizza

1½ cups crushed tomatoes
1 teaspoon dried oregano
1 teaspoon dried basil
2 tablespoons grated Romano
cheese

5 (1-ounce) slices mozzarella
cheese
5 (1-ounce) slices provolone
cheese
2 ounces pepperoni, sliced

1. **Make the pizza dough:** In the bowl of a stand mixer, dissolve the yeast with the hot water and sugar. Let it stand for about 5 minutes until the yeast is activated.

2. Attach the dough hook to the mixer and stir in the olive oil. Add the flour and salt and mix on medium speed for 4 minutes, or until the dough is smooth and pliable. Turn the dough out of the bowl onto a work surface and knead by hand for about 2 minutes.

3. Coat a deep bowl with a tablespoon of olive oil and place the ball of dough in it, turning to coat all sides. Cover the bowl with plastic wrap and a clean kitchen towel. Let it sit in a draft-free area for 2 hours.

4. After it is risen, do not punch it down. Transfer it to a 12-inch deep-dish pizza pan or cake pan. Press the dough over the bottom of the pan and up the sides. Set the pan aside.

5. **Make the pepperoni pizza:** Position a rack in the center of the oven and preheat to 475°F.

6. In a bowl, combine the crushed tomatoes, oregano, basil, and Romano.

7. Lay the slices of mozzarella and provolone on top of the dough, covering all of the dough. Spread the tomato mixture evenly over the cheese layer. Arrange the sliced pepperoni over the tomato sauce.

8. Bake the pizza in the center of the oven for 20 to 25 minutes, or until the crust is golden and pulls away from the sides of the pan.

9. Let the pizza rest a few minutes, then cut into wedges with a pizza wheel.

Makes 8 servings

Instead of pepperoni, try roasted chicken or cooked sausage. You can also finish your pizza with a shower of fresh basil in season.

UNO PIZZERIA & GRILL
Pizza Skins

THIS CLEVER IDEA FROM UNO'S IS THE PERFECT PARTY APPETIZER. USE A STORE-BOUGHT PIZZA CRUST AND LEFTOVER MASHED POTATOES TO MAKE THEIR VERSION OF A LOADED POTATO SKIN.

1 cup mashed potatoes
1 (12-inch) prebaked crust, such as Boboli
½ cup shredded Cheddar cheese

½ cup crumbled crisp-cooked bacon
2 green onions, chopped

Toppings
Sliced black olives
Sour cream
Salsa
Guacamole

Sliced jalapeño peppers
Tomatoes
Fried onions

1. Preheat the oven to 350°F.
2. Spread the mashed potatoes over the bottom of the pizza crust and bake until warmed throughout.
3. Sprinkle with the Cheddar and bacon. Return to the oven and bake until the cheese is melted.
4. Sprinkle with the green onions. Serve as is, or with any of your favorite toppings.

Makes 6 servings

This is a good recipe to make with the kids—it's not too hard, and they'll get to taste the results of their labor within minutes.

RESOURCES

1. Baby Center, "Nutrition Guidelines for Young Children" (web article)
   www.babycenter.com/0_nutrition-guidelines-for-young-children_9245
   .bc?page=2

2. Center for Disease Control (CDC), "Childhood Obesity Facts" (web article)
   www.cdc.gov/healthyyouth/obesity/facts.htm

3. Children's Hunger Alliance, Child Care Provider Resources
   www.childrenshungeralliance.org/index.cfm?fuseaction=cms
   .page&id=1038

4. Child Nutrition Programs, USDA Directory by State
   www.fns.usda.gov/cnd/Contacts/StateDirectory.htm

5. Choose My Plate, "Physical Activity" (web article)
   www.choosemyplate.gov/physical-activity/amount.html

6. Family Education, "Nutrition for Toddlers and Preschoolers" (web article)
   life.familyeducation.com/nutrition-and-diet/growth-and-development/
   44302.html

7. Info Please, "Fat and Calorie Content of Fast Food versus a Home
   Cooked Meal" (Infographic)
   www.infoplease.com/ipa/A0934642.html#ixzz36zxnNJFp

8. Kids Eat Great, "Sneaky Ways with Veggies" (web article)
   www.kidseatgreat.com/sneaky-ways-with-veggies/

9. Kids Eat Right, "Portion Distortion" (web article)
   www.eatright.org/resource/food/nutrition/dietary-guidelines-and-my
   plate/portion-distortion

10. KidsHealth, "Keeping Portions Under Control" (web article)
    kidshealth.org/parent/nutrition_center/healthy_eating/portions.html

11. "Family Meals" (web article)
    kidshealth.org/parent/nutrition_center/healthy_eating/family_meals.html

12. Kids Want to Know, "Why Is Healthy Eating So Important" (web article)
    www.kidshealth.org/kid/stay_healthy/body/poll_health_literacy.html

13. Let's Move, "Learn the Facts" (web article)
www.letsmove.gov/learn-facts/epidemic-childhood-obesity

14. Live Strong, "The Importance of Healthy Eating in Children" (web article)
www.livestrong.com/article/74307-importance-eating-children/

15. Mayo Clinic, "Healthy recipes: A guide to ingredient substitutions" (web article)
www.mayoclinic.org/healthy-living/nutrition-and-healthy-eating/in-depth/healthy-recipes/art-20047195

16. "Nutrition and Healthy Eating" (web article)
www.mayoclinic.org/healthy-living/nutrition-and-healthy-eating/in-depth/healthy-cooking/art-20049346?pg=2

17. Medline Plus, "Age-Appropriate Diet for Children" (web article)
www.nlm.nih.gov/medlineplus/ency/article/002455.htm

18. Medscape, "Stop the Pop: Soda Linked to Aggression, Inattention in Kids" (web article)
www.medscape.com/viewarticle/809767

19. *New York Times*, "Is Junk Food Really Cheaper?" (opinion article)
www.nytimes.com/2011/09/25/opinion/sunday/is-junk-food-really-cheaper.html?_r=3&pagewanted=all&

20. *Shape*, "The 5 Healthiest Ways to Cook" (web article)
www.shape.com/healthy-eating/cooking-ideas/5-healthiest-ways-cook

21. WebMD, "How Much Sleep Do Children Need?" (web article)
www.webmd.com/parenting/guide/sleep-children

22. WebMD, "Your Child's Nutrition: The Power of Parents" (web article)
www.webmd.com/children/features/your-childs-nutrition-power-parents

TRADEMARKS

- Applebee's is a registered trademark of Applebee's International, Inc.
- Arby's is a registered trademark of Arby's Restaurant Group, Inc.
- Auntie Anne's is a registered trademark of FOCUS Brands Inc.
- Baskin-Robbins is a registered trademark of Baskin-Robbins.
- Ben & Jerry's is a registered trademark of Ben & Jerry's Homemade, Inc.
- Benihana is a registered trademark of Benihana, Inc.
- Bennigan's is a registered trademark of Bennigan's Grill & Tavern.
- Bertucci's is a registered trademark of Bertucci's Corporation.
- Bob Evans is a registered trademark of Bob Evans Farms, Inc.
- Bonefish Grill is a registered trademark of Bonefish Grill, LLC.
- Boston Market is a registered trademark of Boston Market Corporation, which is a wholly owned subsidiary of McDonald's Corporation.
- Bubba Gump Shrimp Co. is a registered trademark of Bubba Gump Shrimp Co.
- Buca di Beppo is a registered trademark of Planet Hollywood International, Inc.
- Burger King is a registered trademark of Burger King Corporation.
- Cafe Rio is a registered trademark of Cafe Rio, Inc.
- California Pizza Kitchen is a registered trademark of California Pizza Kitchen, Inc.
- Charley's is a registered trademark of Gosh Enterprises, Inc.
- The Cheesecake Factory is a registered trademark of The Cheesecake Factory, Inc.
- Chevys Fresh Mex is a registered trademark of Chevys Inc.
- Chick-fil-A is a registered trademark of CFA Properties, Inc.
- Chili's is a registered trademark of Brinker International.
- Chipotle Mexican Grill is a registered trademark of Chipotle's Grill, Inc.

- Cinnabon is a registered trademark of Cinnabon, Inc.
- Claim Jumper is a registered trademark of Landry's, Inc.
- Cold Stone Creamery is a registered trademark of Kahala, LLC.
- Copeland's is a registered trademark of Al Copeland Investments, Inc.
- Cracker Barrel is a registered trademark of CBOCS Properties, Inc.
- Dairy Queen is a registered trademark of Dairy Queen, Inc., and Berkshire Hathaway, Inc.
- Dave & Buster's is a registered trademark of Dave & Buster's.
- Denny's is a registered trademark of DFO, LLC.
- Domino's is a registered trademark of Domino's IP Holder LLC.
- Dunkin' Donuts is a registered trademark of DD IP Holder LLC.
- Famous Dave's is a registered trademark of Famous Dave's of America, Inc.
- Fatburger is a registered trademark of Fatburger Inc.
- Five Guys is a registered trademark of Five Guys Holdings, LLC.
- Friendly's is a registered trademark of Friendly's Ice Cream, LLC.
- Golden Corral is a registered trademark of Golden Corral Corporation.
- IHOP is a registered trademark of International House of Pancakes Inc.
- Jamba Juice is a registered trademark of Jamba Juice Company.
- Joe's Crab Shack is a registered trademark of Landry's Seafood Restaurants, Inc.
- Johnny Carino's is a registered trademark of Fired Up, Inc.
- KFC is a registered trademarks of Yum! Brands, Inc.
- Krispy Kreme is a registered trademark of Krispy Kreme Doughnut Corporation.
- Lofthouse is a registered trademark of ConAgra Foods, Inc.
- McDonald's is a registered trademark of the McDonald's Corporation.
- The Melting Pot is a registered trademark of The Melting Pot Restaurants, Inc.
- Old Spaghetti Factory is a registered trademark of The Dussin Group.
- Olive Garden is a registered trademark of Darden Restaurants, Inc.
- Outback Steakhouse is a registered trademark of Outback Steakhouse, Inc.

- Panda Express is a registered trademark of Panda Restaurant Group, Inc.
- Panera Bread is a registered trademark of Panera Bread.
- Pepperidge Farm is a registered trademark of Pepperidge Farm, Incorporated.
- P.F. Chang's is a registered trademark of P.F. Chang's China Bistro, Inc.
- Red Lobster is a registered trademark of Darden Restaurants, Inc.
- Red Robin is a registered trademark of Red Robin International, Inc.
- Ruby Tuesday is a registered trademark of Morrison Restaurants, Inc.
- Sonic is a registered trademark of America's Drive-In Brand Properties LLC.
- Starbucks is a registered trademark of Starbucks Corporation.
- Steak 'n Shake is a registered trademark of Steak 'n Shake.
- Subway is a registered trademark of Doctor's Associates, Inc.
- TGI Fridays is a registered trademark of T.G.I. Fridays, Inc.
- Uno Pizzeria & Grill is a registered trademark of Pizzeria Uno Corporation.

RESTAURANT WEBSITES

To find a restaurant near you, please visit:

Applebee's	www.applebees.com
Arby's	www.arbys.com
Auntie Anne's	www.auntieannes.com
Baskin-Robbins	www.baskinrobbins.com
Ben & Jerry's	www.benjerry.com
Benihana	www.benihana.com
Bennigan's	www.bennigans.com
Bertucci's	www.bertuccis.com
Bob Evans	www.bobevans.com
Bonefish Grill	www.bonefishgrill.com
Boston Market	www.bostonmarket.com
Bubba Gump Shrimp Co.	www.bubbagump.com
Buca di Beppo	www.bucadibeppo.com
Burger King	www.bk.com
Cafe Rio	www.caferio.com
California Pizza Kitchen	www.cpk.com
Charley's Grilled Subs	www.charleys.com
Cheddar's	www.cheddars.com
The Cheesecake Factory	www.thecheesecakefactory.com
Chevys Fresh Mex	www.chevys.com
Chick-fil-A	www.chick-fil-a.com
Chili's	www.chilis.com
Chipotle Mexican Grill	www.chipotle.com
Cinnabon	www.cinnabon.com
Claim Jumper	www.claimjumper.com
Cold Stone Creamery	www.coldstonecreamery.com
Copeland's	www.copelandsofneworleans.com
Cracker Barrel	www.crackerbarrel.com
Dairy Queen	www.dairyqueen.com
Dave & Buster's	www.daveandbusters.com

Denny's	www.dennys.com
Domino's	www.dominos.com
Dunkin' Donuts	www.dunkindonuts.com
Famous Dave's	www.famousdaves.com
Fatburger	www.fatburger.com
Five Guys	www.fiveguys.com
Friendly's	www.friendlys.com
Golden Corral	www.goldencorral.com
IHOP	www.ihop.com
Jamba Juice	www.jambajuice.com
Joe's Crab Shack	www.joescrabshack.com
Johnny Carino's	www.carinos.com
KFC	www.kfc.com
Krispy Kreme	www.krispykreme.com
Lofthouse	www.lofthousecookies.com
McDonald's	www.mcdonalds.com
The Melting Pot	www.meltingpot.com
Old Spaghetti Factory	www.osf.com
Olive Garden	www.olivegarden.com
Outback Steakhouse	www.outback.com
Panda Express	www.pandaexpress.com
Panera Bread	www.panerabread.com
Pepperidge Farm	www.pepperidgefarm.com
P.F. Chang's	www.pfchangs.com
Red Lobster	www.redlobster.com
Red Robin	www.redrobin.com
Ruby Tuesday	www.rubytuesday.com
Sonic	www.sonicdrivein.com
Starbucks	www.starbucks.com
Steak 'n Shake	www.steaknshake.com
Subway	www.subway.com
TGI Fridays	www.fridays.com
Uno Pizzeria & Grill	www.unos.com

INDEX